TECHNICAL REPORT

A Computational Model of Public Support for Insurgency and Terrorism

A Prototype for More-General Social-Science Modeling

Paul K. Davis • Angela O'Mahony

Prepared for the Office of the Secretary of Defense

RAND NATIONAL DEFENSE RESEARCH INSTITUTE

The research described in this report was prepared for the Office of the Secretary of Defense (OSD). The research was conducted within the RAND National Defense Research Institute, a federally funded research and development center sponsored by OSD, the Joint Staff, the Unified Combatant Commands, the Navy, the Marine Corps, the defense agencies, and the defense Intelligence Community under Contract W74V8H-06-C-0002.

Library of Congress Cataloging-in-Publication Data

Davis, Paul K., 1943-
A computational model of public support for insurgency and terrorism : a prototype for more-general social-science modeling / Paul K. Davis, Angela O'Mahony.
pages cm
Includes bibliographical references.
ISBN 978-0-8330-7919-0 (pbk. : alk. paper)
1. Terrorism—Public opinion. 2. Insurgency—Public opinion. 3. Terrorism—Prevention.
I. O'Mahony, Angela. II. Title..

HV6431.D297 2013
303.6'2501—dc23

2013013214

Published 2013 by the RAND Corporation
1776 Main Street, P.O. Box 2138, Santa Monica, CA 90407-2138
1200 South Hayes Street, Arlington, VA 22202-5050
4570 Fifth Avenue, Suite 600, Pittsburgh, PA 15213-2665
RAND URL: http://www.rand.org/
To order RAND documents or to obtain additional information, contact
Distribution Services: Telephone: (310) 451-7002;
Fax: (310) 451-6915; Email: order@rand.org

Preface

This report documents an uncertainty-sensitive computational model of public support for insurgency and terrorism, one intended as a prototype illustration of a new and more-general modeling approach. The report is intended primarily for a technical audience of modelers and analysts, and those who commission or manage such activities, but it is only one product of a larger research activity to inform decisionmaking and to be of interest to scholarly audiences. The report builds on prior publications, especially two RAND monographs:

> Paul K. Davis and Kim Cragin (eds.) (2009), *Social Science for Counterterrorism: Putting the Pieces Together.*
>
> Paul K. Davis, Eric Larson, Zachary Haldeman, Mustafa Oguz, and Rashodhara Rana (2012), *Understanding and Influencing Public Support for Insurgency and Terrorism.*

The research described here was sponsored by the Office of Naval Research and the Human Social, Cultural, and Behavioral Modeling (HSCB) program of the Department of Defense, with supplementary funding by the U.S. Marine Corps Combat Development Center. This research was conducted within the Acquisition and Technology Policy Center of the RAND National Defense Research Institute, a federally funded research and development center sponsored by the Office of the Secretary of Defense, the Joint Staff, the Unified Combatant Commands, the Navy, the Marine Corps, the defense agencies, and the defense Intelligence Community. Comments and suggestions are welcome and should be addressed to the authors in RAND's Santa Monica office (pdavis@rand.org; aomahon1@rand.org).

For more information on the RAND Acquisition and Technology Policy Center, see http://www.rand.org/nsrd/ndri/centers/atp.html or contact the director (contact information is provided on the web page).

Contents

Figures

Tables

Summary

Overview

This report is part of a longer-term research agenda that began with a 2008–2009 RAND study reviewing and integrating social-science knowledge related to counterterrorism. That study used qualitative conceptual causal models called "factor trees" to show compactly all the different factors contributing to various aspects of terrorism at a slice in time and how the factors relate to each other qualitatively. That work reflected a considerable base of social-science knowledge. In the 2009–2011 period, the factor trees were subsequently tested and refined in empirical studies; they were also used in a variety of applications.

This report describes a next step. Going beyond the conceptual and qualitative, we have specified and implemented a prototype *computational* model (PSOT) for just one of the earlier factor-tree models, that addressing public support of terrorism and insurgency. The earlier model is extensively discussed in Davis, Larson, et al., 2012. The factor tree itself is shown in Figure S.1. Our prototype seeks to describe, as a function of contributing factors, the extent to which a nation's public supports an ongoing insurgency and its use of terrorism. The support may involve, for example, sympathy, approval, material contributions, sheltering from the government, or direct participation in insurgent operations. Public support is a complicated aggregation because "the public" is often heterogeneous with numerous disputing factions. Moreover, public support is not a purely "rational" behavior predictable with a stable utility function.* We undertook building a computational model with trepidation because characterizing the mathematics of how factors *combine* required going well beyond the established science base.

Approach. Our approach to modeling is systemic and causal, rather than statistical as in much social science. In contrast to most computational modeling, we emphasize transparency and explicit treatment of uncertainty. We *routinely* show model results as a function of parameters, thereby making results contingent on contexts and assumptions. This is quite different from the norm of constructing a single model treated as though it were "correct," constructing an approved database for all the input assumptions, running the model, and reporting the results as a point prediction (perhaps with minor sensitivity testing). That is, it is different from treating the model as an "answer machine."

Static Versus Dynamic. Factor trees and our prototype model are aggregate-level static models intended to (1) sharpen and clarify knowledge elicitation; (2) improve the coherence of discussion assessing and diagnosing a situation; and, more qualitatively, (3) to improve the ability to reason about how change in the situation can come about and what factors might

* Such issues and subtleties are discussed in Davis, Larson, et al. (2012). They are not repeated here.

be correspondingly influenced. These models are not themselves dynamic; that is, they do not predict changes over time, although they do provide a partial language for discussing change. As discussed in Davis, Larson, et al. (2012), we urge users of these static aggregate-level models to complement them with influence-diagram and system-dynamic methods that focus on time dependence, and with models that delve more deeply into faction-level dynamics within a complex society. The aggregate-level static models, however, are very useful first steps in themselves, especially to aid higher-level reasoning.

Character of Report. This report is inherently technical, analytic, and even mathematical: After all, it explains and documents a computer model. Nonetheless, our intent has been to maintain close contact with the social-science phenomena and understandable qualitative theory, rather than becoming lost in mathematical and programming details. We intend that the report's primary concepts be accessible to a broad range of readers, while also providing the rigorous detail necessary for modelers and analysts.

Finally, we emphasize that the report describes a prototype model illustrating concretely a new approach. The prototype model itself should be seen not as a definitive end point, but rather as a serious straw man to be reviewed, debated, and improved upon.

The Research Challenges

The conceptual factor-tree model for the prototype is shown in Figure S.1. If an arrow points from one variable (factor) to another, it means that more of the former tends to increase the latter if the influence is positive (the + sign is omitted by default). If the arrow bears a negative sign, then more of the former tends to decrease the latter. If the arrow bears a "+/–" sign, then even the direction of the influence is uncertain.

The tree includes tens of factors, but they are arranged in layers because most factors have their effect through higher-level factors. Technically, this is multiresolution modeling; it also reflects the way humans routinely reason.

In Figure S.1, the highest-level factors are connected by "~ands," implying that the top-level effect depends to a first approximation on *all* of those factors being present. In contrast, the lower-level factors are combined with "ors" (implying that the higher effect depends on some combination of the lower-level effects, with no one of them being necessary). For a particular country at a particular time, the influences in a factor tree may have influence arrows of varied thickness to indicate that some are more important than others (not illustrated in Figure S.1).

Some factors, shown at the bottom of the figure, are cross-cutting. For example, if the United States were drawn into a new war in the Middle East, that would probably affect the subsequent values of numerous factors in the tree itself. Some of these cross-factors can be seen as environmental; others relate to culture and emotions.

Building a computational model based on a factor tree posed numerous challenges, as summarized in Table S.1. This list guided our research. The challenges were in four blocks, as indicated by shading in the table: (1) defining the factors and their values; (2) defining how to reflect cryptic factor-tree "and" and "or" relationships, ambiguous influences indicated by +/– signs, and the varied significance of influences sometimes indicated by arrow thickness (illustrated in the text, but not Figure S.1); (3) dealing with uncertainty about factor values and combining rules, and showing results of exploratory analysis across uncertainties; and

Figure S.1
Conceptual Model for Public Support of Insurgency and Terrorism

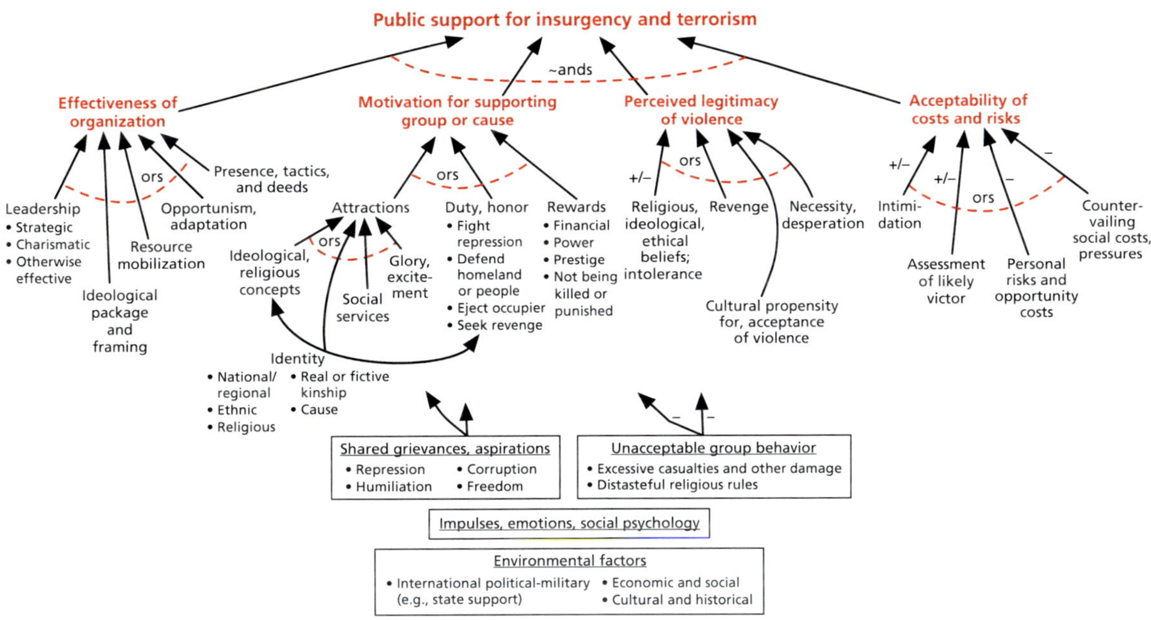

NOTES: Applies at a snapshot in time. Current factor values can affect future values of some or all other factors.
RAND *TR1220-S.1*

Table S.1
Challenges and Issues

Challenge	Issues
Define factors and factor values	How many values are sufficient? How can soft and fuzzy variables be reasonably defined?
Define "and" connections mathematically	How rigid should the relationship be? How can uncertainties be reflected?
Define "or" connections mathematically	How many alternative functional relationships are needed?
Define ambiguous and conflicting influences (+/– signs) mathematically	What does the ambiguity mean? How can it be represented?
Represent implications of line thickness in factor trees	How should relative importance of factors be understood and represented in the model?
Represent uncertainty of factor values	Should this be done by giving ranges of parameter values or by using probabilistic methods?
Represent structural uncertainty of combining relationships	Should this be done with alternative models, structural parameterization, or both?
Build model for exploratory analysis under uncertainty	How should far-reaching exploratory analysis be accomplished? When should probabilistic methods be used?
Assess "confidence" of nominal factor-value estimates and of model outputs	How should this best be accomplished?
Implement model in understandable high-level language	What language? How can the model be made transparent, comprehensible, and easy to re-implement (a form of reuse)?

(4) implementing the model in a computer program in which substantive content is transparent, comprehensible, and as language-independent as possible so as to facilitate model re-use, model composition, or rapid reprogramming.

Our Solutions to the Challenges

An important element of the research was identifying logical/mathematical relationships to express the intended social-science knowledge and uncertainty. For the problem treated by the prototype—and hopefully for a broader class of social-science problems—we found a minimal set of mathematical building-block methods that seemed sufficient. We present these methods as hypotheses to be reviewed and tested empirically by methods of social psychology and political science. Briefly, the methods we suggest are as follows.

Defining Factors and Their Values

It is often comfortable and natural when discussing social issues to use qualitative values such as "Very Low" or "Very High," so we constructed much of PSOT's interface accordingly. In doing so, we had to keep track of whether, e.g., a "Very High" influence was positive or negative. Values within the model are represented numerically on a continuous scale from –10 to 10, but a discrete set of corresponding qualitative values can be used instead, with 1, 3, 5, 7, and 9 corresponding to Very Low, Low, Medium, High, and Very High (with the influences being either positive or negative). A truncated set can be used with 3, 5, and 7 corresponding to Low, Medium, and High. Precisely what these values *mean* depends on the particular problem, but they must be approximately "equally spaced" rather than merely indicating relative order. To establish meaning, we take the common qualitative social-science approach of defining by example using short narratives. How values can be estimated by convenient measurements is a general and context-dependent challenge outside the scope of this report. In particular settings, a given factor's value may be well approximated by something as concrete as polling results, but in other cases that same class of data will be misleading or unavailable.

Combining Relationships

Factors Combining by "~and" Relationships. How should we represent an "~and" relationship? If factors were binary, with values of 1 (present) or 0 (not present), the mathematics would be as in elementary logic. However, with factors that can have values such as Low, Medium, or High, the issue becomes more subtle. We represent approximate "and" relationships with *thresholded* linear weighted sums, which allow for such nonlinearities as critical-mass phenomena. In this approach, the higher-level effect (e.g., public support) is assessed as small unless all of the contributing factors reach or exceed their threshold values, in which case a linear weighted sum can be used. If all thresholds are set to their least-demanding levels, the relationship reduces to a simple linear weighted sum.

Factors Combining with "or" Relationships. We found it sufficient to distinguish between two starkly different kinds of "or" relationships:

1. Primary Factors: The effect depends on the largest factor, with possible adjustment by a second factor.

2. Thresholded Linear Weighted Sums: Factors that exceed their threshold are combined linearly; using thresholded linear weighted sums allows for both dilution and reinforcement.

Which is most apt will be context-dependent, but one or the other will be sufficient in a wide range of contexts. That is, the mathematical toolkit need not be too large.

Factors with Ambiguous Influence (+/– signs). Factor trees use +/– to indicate that the directionality of an influence is uncertain. We distinguished between two very different reasons:

1. Stochastic Behavior: The influence's sign is effectively random because the underlying factors in conflict are unknown, unobservable, rapidly changing, or some combination.
2. Conflicting Influences: The influence is the result of two or more understandable conflicting lower-level influences, such as might occur when two population factions have opposite positions on an issue (in the prototype effort, we did not consider larger numbers of factions). Enough may be known to represent these and to estimate their resolution.

We reflect effective randomness by considering the input to be uncertain and either showing results for both cases (deterministic analysis) or treating the factor probabilistically. For conflicting influences, we use a function that assumes that the stronger of the sub-influences *largely* determines the result, but with the degree of domination controlled by an uncertain parameter.

Again, we emphasize that there is no single "correct" mathematical function for these several combining relationships. The actual combined effect will depend on context and sometimes on microscopic history. For example, in a particular situation, the dominant faction's perspective may altogether dominate because recent bad blood between leadership factions has made any other outcome untenable. The opposite could also occur, where personal relations and recent history makes compromise appropriate and feasible. Sometimes, but only sometimes, will experts know enough about such matters to make reasonable conjectures about which algorithm is more apt.

The toolkit of combining relationships that we settled on can be regarded as hypotheses about combining relationships to be tested in psychological research and case studies, both to determine the adequacy of the choices we provide and to better understand when one applies rather than another (e.g., When are threshold effects stronger and weaker? When does the strongest factor altogether dominate?).

Representing Uncertainty

We designed PSOT for exploratory analysis under multidimensional uncertainty (i.e., analysis that shows results for all combinations of the relevant factor values). We prefer to do exploratory analysis deterministically—establishing a discrete range of plausible values for each input, running all the possible combination cases, and then looking for patterns indicating what combinations of factor values lead to results that are good, bad, or indifferent. The analyst and decisionmaker can then make judgments about the relative plausibility of the different domains before reaching conclusions or taking actions. This approach has been used by RAND in many studies over the past two decades in connection with planning for adaptiveness and robust decisionmaking.

We also use an alternative approach that characterizes each input with a probability distribution and generates a probability distribution for results. This is sometimes appropriate and valuable, but can obfuscate causal relationships and be seriously misleading if correlations are ignored. If there are numerous uncertain factors, then it is sometimes best to use the hybrid approach of treating the most important of them deterministically while treating the others stochastically.

When probabilistic methods are appropriate, we use several methods:

Stochastic Functions. For probabilistic work, we used triangular distributions and Monte Carlo sampling. The triangular distribution represents asymmetric uncertainties, is readily understood by non-mathematician experts, and connects well to a "most likely" value. The analyst may increase the uncertainty range beyond what experts suggest because empirical evidence indicates that experts routinely underestimate the probability of low-probability events.

Correlations. It is incorrect to assume independent probabilities for many of the factors appearing in models such as ours. Attempting to model correlational details among numerous variables, however, would not be justified by the available knowledge and would complicate both interaction with experts and analysis. Thus, we adopted a parametric approach correlating a bundle of factors with a single variable parameter. This is sufficient to assess the significance of correlations to results.

Assessing Confidence. Uncertainty analysis can generate not only "expected value" or "mean" results, but also confidence intervals. Those can be based on deterministic or probabilistic calculations, as above. The inputs for the estimates may be made at different levels of detail. Confidence estimates are often more trustworthy and humbling if based on holistic expert judgment or historical information, rather than detailed calculations reflecting only specific known uncertainties.

Implementation

We wanted to implement the model in a way that would permit substantive review, re-use, and composability (using the model in combination with others). With this in mind, we used the high-level programming language Analytica. The model's content can be largely comprehended without dealing with programming issues. The model is expressed visually (in influence diagrams) and, at the next level of detail, in a relatively simple syntax closely tied to mathematics rather than procedural programming. The result is intuitive for those with some background with vectors, matrices, and arrays. This tie to mathematics also makes the model especially suitable as a specification model available to researchers generally.

Exploratory Analysis to Understand Context- and Assumption-Dependency

Our study reports model building rather than analysis, but we illustrate exploratory analysis over uncertainty. Figure S.2 shows PSOT results for the extent to which "the public" will regard the costs and risks of supporting the insurgency and its terrorism as acceptable. That is, what combinations of factors would create a net sense of unacceptable costs (such factors are colored green in Figure S.2, because they are good from the counterinsurgency perspective) or low costs (shown in red)? Results are shown as a function of five factors: (1) intimida-

Figure S.2
Illustrative Exploratory Analysis: How Public Support for Insurgency Depends on Five Uncertain Factors

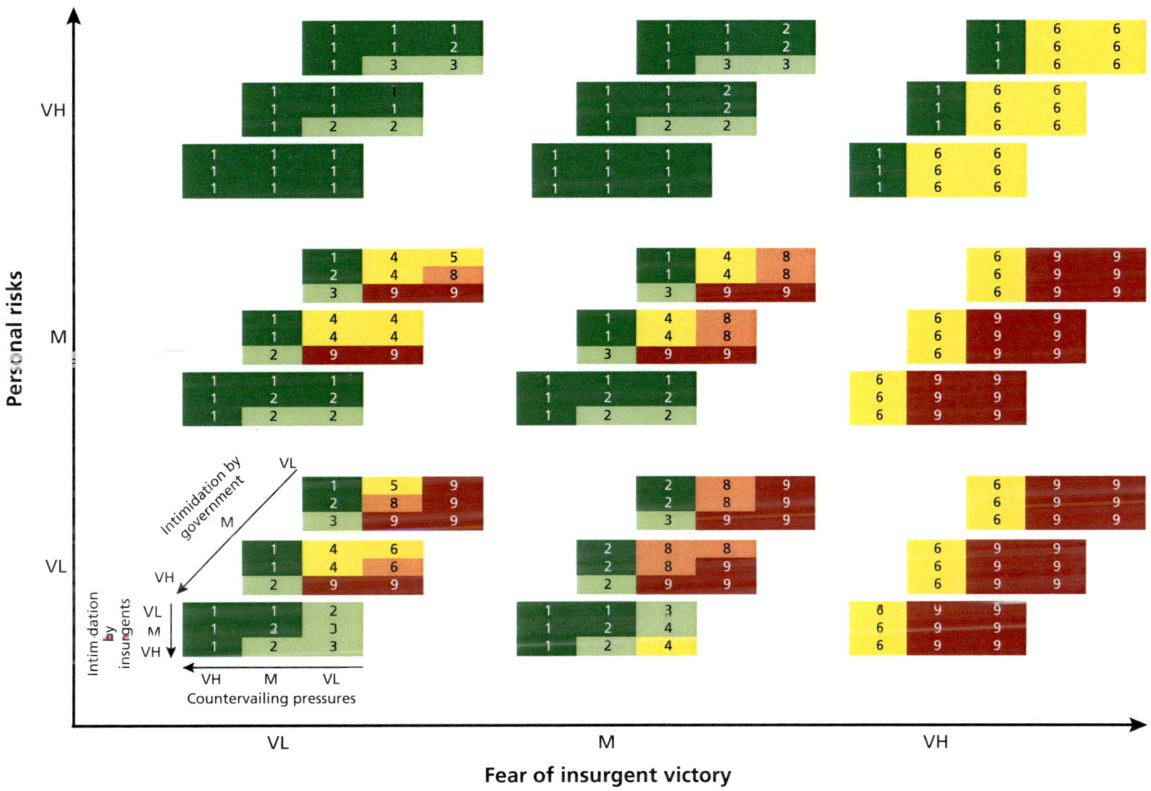

NOTES: The numbers shown are the values used internally in PSOT. Because low acceptability of costs and risks is good for the counterinsurgent side, the colors for 1, 3, 5, 7, and 9 are green, light green, yellow, orange, and red, respectively.
RAND *TR1220-S.2*

tion by the insurgents, which raises acceptability of support by making it dangerous to *not* support the insurgency; (2) intimidation by the government; (3) fear that the insurgents will win; (4) countervailing social pressures (e.g., the urgings of family respected leaders not to provide support; and (5) other personal costs of support. Figure S.2 reflects the Primary Factors approach mentioned above.

Such a depiction can help in diagnosing the seriousness of a situation, discussing what factors must be changed to move to a better situation, and assessing the relative leverage of factors (which may or may not be subject to influence). The model, then, is not about prediction, but about improved diagnosis and reasoning. It can be especially valuable in dampening enthusiasms when one factor is subject to influence but the net effect is unlikely to be significant, or in suggesting approaches in which moderate influence on two or more factors may have synergistic favorable effects.

Conclusions and Next Steps

The prototype effort demonstrated the potential for markedly improving representation of social-science knowledge, eliciting knowledge from subject-matter experts, dealing with uncertainty, and working on the components of more or less composable models. Next steps should include the following:

- Experimentation *using* the prototype model for reviews, substantive discussion, knowledge elicitation, and exploratory analysis for particular applications, such as understanding data from Afghanistan, Iraq, or Yemen.
- Working with government offices to create efficient processes for exposing such models to peer review by the scholarly and operational communities, after which revised versions could be considered as vetted "modules" for model composition.
- Building analogous "specification models" for other aspects of terrorism, insurgency, and irregular warfare. Each could be used on its own or become a module in more comprehensive system models.
- Extending the methods to other social-science domains.

Social science is notoriously difficult—and, as the cliché goes, much "harder" than the hard sciences. Nonetheless, social science contains extraordinary amounts of knowledge. Our report is one step in the process of learning how to better represent that knowledge in increasingly rigorous, albeit often qualitative and uncertainty-sensitive, systemic models.

As a final comment, an enormous amount of information has been gathered over the past decade regarding both insurgency and terrorism. However, it has not come together well, and the potential exists for the information to vanish with time and new priorities. If the knowledge is to be captured and expressed coherently, before memories fade and data disappear, models like PSOT could prove quite valuable because they can be individually understood, reviewed, debated, and put on the shelf (while maintaining their flexibility and treatment of uncertainty).

Acknowledgments

Our research benefited greatly from an earlier study of terrorism modeling using RAND's internal research and development funds and from extensive discussions about insurgency and terrorism with RAND colleagues and many other individuals in the research, analysis, and operational communities. We appreciate comments and suggestions on a draft version by numerous colleagues and careful formal reviews by Professor John Horgan (Pennsylvania State University) and Dr. Brian Jackson (RAND).

Abbreviations

DoD	Department of Defense
IED	improvised explosive device
PF	Primary Factors (an algorithm)
PSOT	Public Support of Terrorism and Insurgency (model)
SIMD	Stronger Influence Mostly Dominates (an algorithm)
TLWS	Thresholded Linear Weighted Sums (an algorithm)
TLWSV	Variant of TLWS (an algorithm)

CHAPTER ONE

Introduction

This report describes and largely documents a prototype computational model that demonstrates how a more qualitative social-science model can be fully specified and implemented in a way that highlights context-dependence and accounts also for many other uncertainties. The prototype, named with the abbreviation PSOT, builds on a previously published qualitative model and deals with public support of insurgency and terrorism. Our primary purpose is to illustrate a more-general approach, but the PSOT model itself is intended as a serious straw man suitable for review, debate, and possible iteration as proves necessary. It draws on substantial prior research (Davis, Larson, et al., 2012), to which readers should refer for more details on the public-support issue per se.

The report is inherently technical and written primarily for social scientists, analysts, and modelers. However, it is only part of a larger research effort to inform policymakers and both military and civilian "operators" involved with counterinsurgency and counterterrorism.

Background

The Larger Agenda to Which the Study Contributes

The larger effort began when the Department of Defense (DoD) asked RAND to review the social science literature bearing on terrorism. DoD was concerned that modeling and analysis nominally addressing these subjects was not obviously well grounded in science, did not incorporate subtleties that scholarly experts considered important, and was impossible to understand because of poor documentation—with model content buried in computer code and sometimes treated as proprietary. Officials sought to go back to basics and understand what social science actually has to say on these matters. Thus, they asked for a critical review of the scientific literature illuminating points of agreement, disagreement, and ambiguity.

The resulting study (Davis and Cragin, 2009) drew on political science, economics, psychology, cultural history, sociology, anthropology, and terrorism-studies literatures. RAND also brought a "system modeling" perspective to the problem. The study benefited from a review panel of some of the nation's most highly regarded scholars on terrorism.*

Synthesizing knowledge proved to be a major challenge. The knowledge base was rich and deep, but fragmented. It also lacked a unifying, systemic, causal theory. This reflected the fact that research papers and books are often specialized according to discipline or the researchers'

* Those contributing suggestions or formal reviews included Eli Berman, John Horgan, Martha Crenshaw, Brian Jenkins, Doug McAdam, Steve Simon, and Mark Stout.

particular interests. Further, social-science research tends to be qualitative or, when quantitative, to be dominated by statistical analysis. This was not a good match for the needs of officials who wish to understand and reason about the complex issues involved in terrorism. Doing so requires a systemic perspective and some understanding of causal relationships, even if shrouded in uncertainty. The study became a first step toward such a systemic understanding. As discussed below, it used qualitative conceptual models called factor trees to pull knowledge together (Davis, 2009a, 2009b). Appendix A reprints a primer on the method (Davis, 2011).

From the study's outset, RAND anticipated longer-term progress in phases, as indicated in Figure 1.1, with the original study being at the top left. That study, it was hoped, would be followed by additional empirical work to validate the conceptual models and, if justified by results, the building of a prototype uncertainty-sensitive computational model for at least one part of the counterterrorism problem (the activity reported on here, indicated in red). We envision extended research, as shown at the bottom of the figure. In the meantime, as indicated on the right of Figure 1.1, applications began soon after publication of the original study in 2009 and should continue in the years ahead.

The following paragraphs provide background from the earlier phases in 2008–2011. After completing that background, we discuss objectives of the current study.

Representing Knowledge Qualitatively with Factor Trees

As mentioned above, a first and unpretentious step toward a more systemic, causal theory was to use qualitative conceptual models to pull together knowledge. These factor trees can be understood at a glance by people from disparate backgrounds. Rather than just highlighting a few important variables, the intent is for the factor trees to be comprehensive in covering the range of factors suggested by experts as important. As with experts in other domains, terrorism experts are excellent in identifying those factors, even though their ability to draw conclusions

Figure 1.1
Intention: A Phased Program of Research

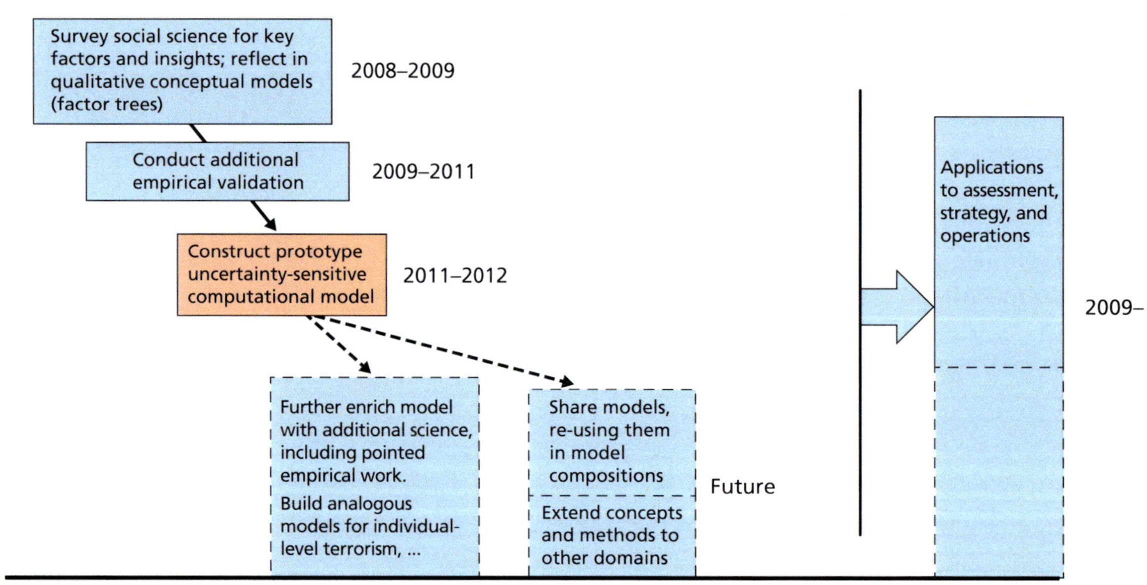

RAND *TR1220-1.1*

and predict future developments is often much less solid (Tetlock, 2005). A factor tree arrays the various factors identified by research, but does not purport to explain precisely how they combine to create effects. This is in distinct contrast with traditional computer models that take precise input assumptions (typically what are thought to be best-guess values) and then predict consequences.

Figure 1.2 shows a slightly modified version of the peer-reviewed generic factor tree that evolved from the original study (Paul, 2009; Davis, Larson, et al., 2012).* The convention is that if an arrow points from one node (i.e., factor) to another, then more of the former tends to cause more of the latter unless the sign on the arrow is negative, in which case more of the former tends to decrease the latter. A "+/–" indicates that the direction of influence is uncertain. Factor trees are related to many other graphical methods, particularly influence diagrams.†

As Figure 1.2 illustrates, factor trees display the factors contributing to a phenomenon in several layers of increasing detail. The phenomenon is described as driven by only a small number of top-level factors, but each of these is affected by lower-level factors, which in turn may be affected by still lower-level factors. This is multiresolution modeling (Davis and Bigelow,

Figure 1.2
Conceptual Model for Public Support of Insurgency and Terrorism

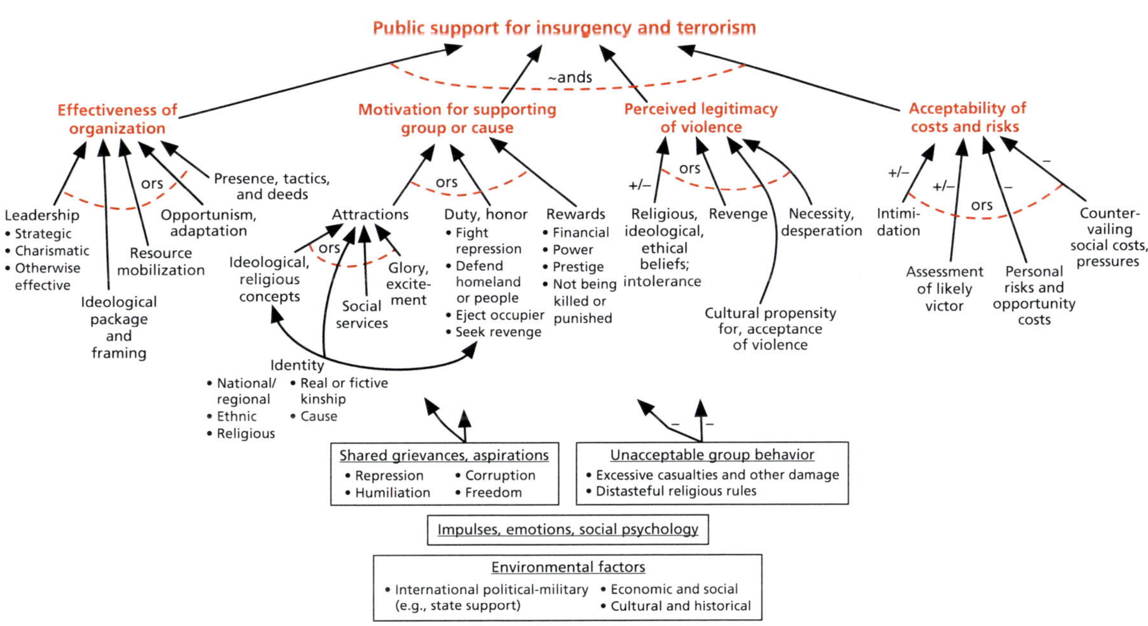

NOTES: Applies at a snapshot in time. Current factor values can affect future values of some or all other factors.
RAND *TR1220-1.2*

---

* Figure 1.2 includes a bulleted item "Not being killed or punished" as an example of Rewards. This had been inadvertently omitted from the first printing of the earlier publication (Davis, Larson, et al., 2012).

† Our factor trees are related to static influence diagrams in policy analysis (Morgan and Henrion, 1992), which were motivated by earlier influence diagrams in decision analysis (Howard and Matheson, 1984; Howard and Matheson, 2005). Except that we suppress dynamics in this particular report, but include information in the form of "ands," "ors," and arrow thickness, our factor trees are also related to causal-loop and stock-flow diagrams of System Dynamics (Forrester, 1963; Sterman, 2000) and to the influence diagrams of "soft operations research" (Rosenhead and Mingers, 2004). They are also related to probabilistic influence diagrams in Bayesian-net/belief-net analysis (Pearl, 2009).

1998). Many of the cause-effect relationships are approximately hierarchical, but others are more cross-cutting (see box at bottom).

Factor trees use "ands" and "ors" as an approximate way to describe how factors affecting a given node relate to each another: Are all of them usually necessary for a higher-level effect to occur, or can various combinations of the subfactors lead to the effect? In the example, the top-level factors are connected by "~ands," i.e., all are necessary to a first approximation, although there can be counter-examples. In other factor trees, some of the arrows have thickened lines to indicate that they are relatively more important. The connection of some factors by "ors" is even more ambiguous. If A and B are connected by an "or," we mean that the result could depend on A, B, or some combination.

Factor trees are useful, but have distinct limitations. Most important, they are *static* models intended for diagnosis and reasoning at a snapshot in time. Subsequently, many factors interact and the result is typically complex; even the concept of causality becomes fuzzy. Accounting for effects and interactions over time is sometimes important and can be accomplished with influence diagrams* or even computational methods such as system dynamic models, agent-based models, or multimodels that combine diverse model types.† Our intent here is to focus on modeling the snapshot-in-time causality. If that is successful, we intend the models to assist in qualitative reasoning about what actions might best be taken to change the situation favorably.

Factor trees have now been used to discuss root causes of terrorism (Noricks, 2009), individual-level movement into terrorism (Helmus, 2009), public support for terrorism (Paul, 2009; Davis, Larson, et al., 2012), the reasoning of terrorist organizations (Jackson, 2009), informing decisions on strategic communication (Davis and Norton, 2011), characterizing prospects for success in stabilization and reconstruction operations (Davis, 2011), and several applied RAND studies for U.S. Special Operations Command (USSOCOM) led by colleagues Kim Cragin, Todd Helmus, and Brian Jackson. They have been used and adapted by the U.S. Marine Corps Combat Development Center in support of military operations.‡

Empirical Testing

The second step in Figure 1.1 was further empirical testing of factor-tree models. The studies by Cragin, Jackson, and Helmus mentioned drew on data from Iraq and Afghanistan. Most recently, RAND completed an empirical study on public support for insurgency and terrorism drawing only on public-source information (Davis, Larson, Haldeman, Oguz, and Rana,

---

* We supplemented factor trees with influence diagrams in a recent study on stabilization and reconstruction (Davis, 2011). Supplementation has also proven valuable in work of the U.S. Marine Corps Combat Development Center in support of operations in Afghanistan.

† Multimodeling experiments on deterrence issues have been led by Kathleen Carley of Carnegie Mellon University and Alec Levis of George Mason University in DoD's Strategic Multilayer Assessment (SMA) program. See, e.g., Carley (2012) and online interdisciplinary research at Carnegie Mellon University (Center for Computational Analysis of Social and Organizational Systems, no date) and George Mason University's System Architectures Laboratory (System Architectures Laboratory, no date). Other multimodeling efforts include BAE Systems' COMPOEX environment, developed under Defense Advanced Research Projects Agency sponsorship; the British Peace Operations Simulation Model (POSM), which has been used in both the United States and Great Britain (Body and Marston, 2011); and research at Georgia Tech's Research Institute (Briscoe et al., 2011).

‡ Private communications with Dr. Michael Bailey and Dr. Robert Sheldon in connection with research for the U.S. Marine Corps Combat Development Command.

2012) for cases involving the Taliban in Afghanistan, debates within al Qaeda and the community of potential supporters, the PKK insurgency in Turkey, and the Maoist insurgency in Nepal. Figure 1.2 is a product of that study. The study focused first on attempts to falsify, as in the version of scientific method suggested by Sir Karl Popper (Popper, 1934), rather than the inductive method associated with Sir Francis Bacon. Second, it sought additional insights to enrich or sharpen the model. This was in the spirit of structured case studies as discussed in Chapter One of a classic book (George and Bennett, 2005). That is, the study sought to improve and enrich an evolving theory, rather than to test statistical correlations.

As it happened, the study uncovered no new factors and found that all of the tree's factors were salient in at least some of the cases. This added credibility to the qualitative theory rather than falsifying it. Further, the study confirmed an important prediction, which was that the relative salience of factors in Figure 1.2 would vary with context. First, the salience of individual factors varied across cases. Religion, for example, played a bigger role in support for al Qaeda than for the PKK. Also, even in a given context, such as the PKK insurgency in Turkey, the relative salience of factors has changed over time as insurgents have adapted their tactics to developments. Marxist-Leninism, for example, has not been much emphasized by the PKK since the collapse of the Soviet Union.

The primary enrichments of the model were to sharpen and highlight the role of *identity*, noting that identity is typically a fundamental factor that affects several higher-level factors in a way that is very difficult and perhaps impossible to disentangle; and to relate organizational effectiveness even more strongly to concepts from social movement theory.

Challenges

Against this background, our report moves from a conceptual factor-tree model to a fully specified, uncertainty-sensitive, modular computational model. Our hope is that such research can improve rigor and nuance, lay the basis for uncertainty analysis, and improve prospects for peer review, sharing, re-use, and model composition.*

Table 1.1 summarizes the challenges of our research project and issues in dealing with them. Its elements constituted the operational plan for our research.

Structure of Report

We address the challenges of Table 1.1 in the remainder of the report. Chapter Two discusses the illustrative factor-tree model in more detail, giving more rigorous and mathematical meaning to its numerous factors and subfactors, how they combine, and how to deal with uncertainty. Although nominally keyed to the specific problem of public support, the mathematical/logical discussion is intended to be more general. Chapter Three describes implementation of Chapter Two's methods in a high-level visual-programming environment. Chapter Four discusses potential applications, drawing on prior experience and the results of some very limited experiments done at the end of the study; it also illustrates how the model can be used for

* The ideas trace back to internally funded RAND research (Davis, 2006; Hillestad and Davis, 2006) and earlier work on "synthetic cognitive models" (National Academy of Sciences, 1996; Davis, 2003b).

Table 1.1
Challenges and Issues: The Basis of the Research Plan

Challenge	Issues
Define factors and factor values	How many values are sufficient? How can soft and fuzzy variables be reasonably defined?
Define "and" connections mathematically	How rigid should the relationship be? How can uncertainties be reflected?
Define "or" connections mathematically	How many alternative functional relationships are needed?
Define ambiguous and conflicting influences (+/– signs) mathematically	What does the ambiguity mean? How can it be represented?
Represent implications of line thickness in factor trees	How should relative importance of factors be understood and represented in the model?
Represent uncertainty of factor values	Should this be done by giving ranges of parameter values or by using probabilistic methods?
Represent structural uncertainty of combining relationships	Should this be done with alternative models, structural parameterization, or both?
Build model for exploratory analysis under uncertainty	How should far-reaching exploratory analysis be accomplished? When should probabilistic methods be used?
Assess "confidence" of nominal factor-value estimates and of model outputs	How should this best be accomplished?
Implement model in understandable high-level language	What language? How can the model be made transparent, comprehensible, and easy to re-implement (a form of reuse)?

exploratory analysis to understand what assumptions and circumstances lead to desirable and undesirable outcomes. Chapter Five draws conclusions from our prototype effort and suggests next steps.

CHAPTER TWO

Specifying the Model

Most of this chapter deals with generic methods that could be useful for a variety of social-science models. However, part of our generic method is starting with the actual problem and defining terms and concepts. Further, it is often easier to discuss methods by illustrating them with specifics rather than using only abstractions. Thus, we proceed by picking up with the factor tree that our prototype built from.

The Conceptual Model

As mentioned in Chapter One, our prototype effort built on a prior factor tree for public support for insurgency and terrorism (Figure 1.2), copied here for convenience as Figure 2.1.

Figure 2.1
The Conceptual Factor-Tree Model

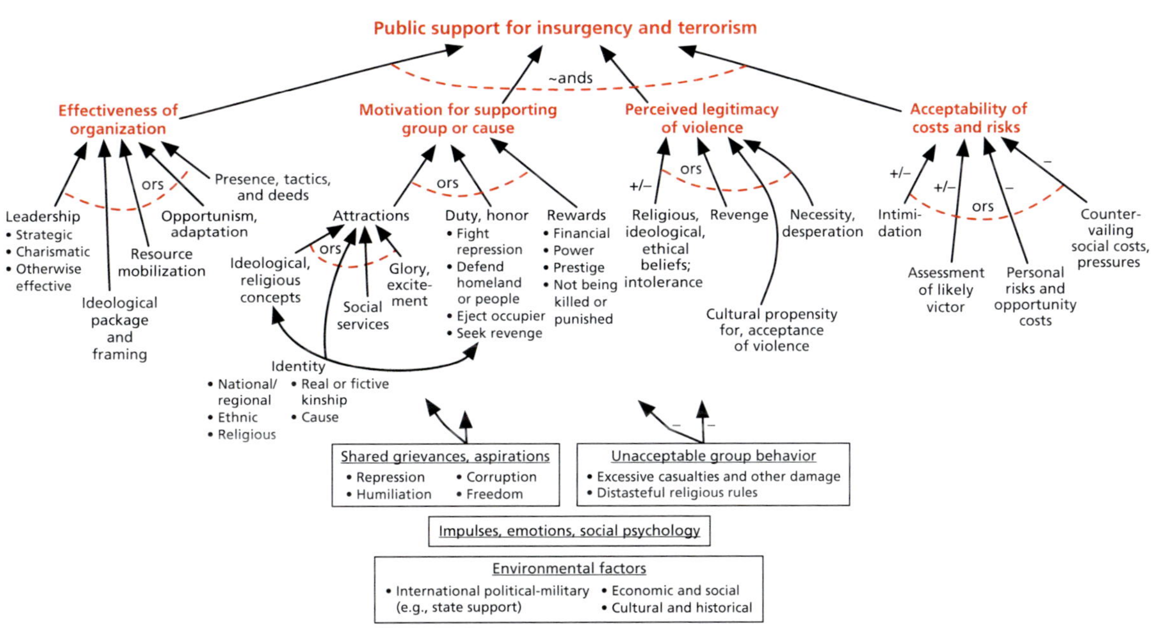

NOTES: Applies at a snapshot in time. Current factor values can affect future values of some or all other factors.
RAND *TR1220-2.1*

The Narrative

Varied definitions of "insurgency" exist, but nearly all assume that the insurgency uses "subversion and violence."* The nature of violence, however, differs greatly across instances, and not all insurgencies make use of terrorism (attacks on noncombatants, such as suicide attacks in markets and other attacks that seek to instill widespread fear). Further, a population may support an insurgency's cause and some of its violence, but may not support and may even oppose terrorism. The issue addressed here, then, is support for *both* insurgency and terrorism (including use of terrorism as a strategy).

The narrative that goes with Figure 2.1 is that public support for insurgency and terrorism depends on four top-level factors: effectiveness of the insurgent organization, motivation to support the insurgency, perceived legitimacy of terrorism, and acceptability of costs and risks (Davis, Larson, et al., 2012). All are necessary to a first approximation as indicated by the "~and" connections.

Organizational Effectiveness

Public support for an insurgent organization requires that the organization exist and have some level of effectiveness. Grievances, identity, and many other individual-level factors are ubiquitous; only sometimes, however, does public support for insurgency build to significant levels. A modicum of organizational effectiveness is ordinarily crucial and may be seen as the result of leadership, ideological package and related framing, the mobilization of resources, opportunism and adaptation to circumstances, and some combination of presence, deeds, and tactics. Over time, this factor also affects and is affected by the other factors.†

Motivation

Most people who support insurgency (or even terrorism) believe that they are doing something positive, such as contributing to a worthy cause, fulfilling a duty, or maintaining honor. Some attractions are rooted in religion or another ideology, a sense of identity, appreciation of social services provided by the organization, the glory and excitement of the cause or activity, or some combination. Referring again to the issue of identity, people may feel a sense of duty or honor to support the insurgency because of nationalism (e.g., when dealing with an occupier) or their connection with a particular ethnic group, tribe, religion, or cause. Other motivations may involve financial payments or gaining power. Still other "motivations" are more negative in character, as when a public supports an insurgency to some extent because it expects the insurgency to succeed, because it is "drawn in" by the action and excitement, or because to not provide support risks death.

In Figure 2.1, strong motivation for the insurgency does not imply acceptance of terrorism. That is the subject of the next factor.

---

* Somewhat different definitions can be found in the *U.S. Government Counterinsurgency Guide*, January 2009, U.S. and British field manuals, and dictionaries. Those differences are of no significance to this report.

† The Arab Spring movement of 2010–2011 did not initially enjoy the benefits of organizational effectiveness, although that had improved by the time of President Mubarak's ouster. The loosely defined organization was at least moderately effective by virtue of shared motivation and anger. It did not have staying power, however, and the Muslim Brotherhood was playing a much bigger role as of June 2012.

Perception of Legitimacy for Violence, Particularly Terrorism

The public in a given nation may strongly support the cause of an insurgency (e.g., Kurdish nationalism or the need to overthrow despotic governments) but be ambivalent about violence. It may support such violence as ambushing an occupier's army or blowing up government arsenals, but may see terrorism (indiscriminate killing of innocent civilians) as illegitimate. One of the observations made in earlier empirical work in Afghanistan was that some people regard terrorism as not only legitimate but required by Islam, while others regard it as fundamentally unIslamic.

Violence and even terrorism may be perceived as legitimate for many reasons. The reasons may be religious, otherwise ideological, or ethical; they may be due to intolerance rooted in unthinking ethnic prejudices and ignorance that denigrate "others"; they may be based in a sense of rightful personal revenge or, in a culture with endemic violence, a belief that legitimacy is a non-issue. And, even if violence is seen as deplorable, it may be seen as necessary. It should be remembered that participants in even "good" revolutions only sometimes have the luxury of taking a relatively peaceful approach as in the Egypt of 2011's Arab Spring. A public that is strongly motivated to support an insurgency as part of a virtuous revolution or resistance against an occupier may nonetheless reject a strategy or terrorism with indiscriminate attacks on noncombatants. In an important variant, a public may be willing to support what amounts to terrorism, but only against those seen as "others." In any case, we should not confuse support for the laying of improvised explosive devices (IEDs) in the path of a military convoy with support for terrorist attacks in public squares.

One of the arrows within Perceived Legitimacy has an ambiguous sign +/– because the influence of religion and ideology can work either to support or undercut terrorism's legitimacy (work by Zachary Haldeman included in Davis, Larson, et al., 2012). Both positive and negative influences may be present simultaneously in a population, or we may simply not know what the influence is or how it will change over time.

Acceptability of Costs and Risks

The fourth branch of the factor tree is expressed as acceptability, given motivations, of costs and risks. This formulation reflects the observation that behaviors are often not the result solely of sober cost-benefit calculations. Rather, they may stem also from such emotions as the excitement of revolution or the horror of having witnessed slaughter. As a result, they need not be what an economist would normally consider to be "rational." Young men and women, of course, are often famously insensitive to risks. Other sources for perceptions of risk include intimidation and a projection of the likely victor. These can work in either direction, as indicated by the ambiguous +/– signs on the influence arrows in Figure 2.1. Both the government and insurgent organization may practice intimidation, and—depending on events—either side may be seen as likely to prevail.* There may also be personal-level risks and opportunities to consider, and a variety of countervailing social and cultural pressures (e.g., the social pressures from family and friends not to get involved, in part because they fear reprisals). All of

* The astute reader will note that intimidation of the population by the insurgents, or the public's perception that the insurgents are likely to be victorious, can also contribute to a grudging version of "motivation" (the Rewards factor in the second branch of the factor tree). This cross linkage is not shown explicitly for simplicity.

these influences may change over time*—in part as the relative strength and immediate presence of government or insurgent forces waxes and wanes. The factor refers to acceptability of costs and risks, rather than costs and risks themselves, because combining rules are easier to discuss when all the influences entering a higher-level node have the same sign.

Cross-Cutting Factors and Effects Over Time

Some "cross-cutting" factors are shown at the bottom of Figure 2.1. Also, the factor of identity, in the middle portion of the figure above the boxes, influences higher-level factors in two separate branches. Identity is often more fundamental than factors such as religion, ideology, or duty and honor, which are difficult to disentangle.

A related issue is that, over time, factors affect each other across branches. For example, one manifestation of an ineffective organization is behavior seen over time as "unacceptable" (one of the lower boxes in Figure 2.1). That, in turn, may affect subsequent values of motivation and perceived legitimacy. For example, al Qaeda's 2003 attacks in Riyadh killed numerous innocents, most of them Muslims, which undercut subsequent public support for al Qaeda. Indeed, in the later years before his death, Osama bin Laden was highly concerned about al Qaeda not repeating the mistakes of its experience in Iraq.† Public sentiment in the Islamic world had turned against al Qaeda because of its tactics, even though it remained highly critical of the United States and its intentions (Kull et al., 2009).

Moving to a Computational Model

The factor tree in Figure 2.1 provides a big-picture view of the factors having causal effects within the system of interest. It does not explain, however, what happens at the various nodes of the tree, except for the cryptic "~ands" and "ors." The intent of the factor tree is to convey simply the most solid knowledge, while not purporting to treat the many subtleties on which social-science knowledge has been uncertain and less coherent. In what follows we provide more such details, but doing so requires going beyond peer-reviewed, settled, social-science knowledge. The details that we specify are informed, however, by a combination of the social-science and psychological literatures, the terrorism and counterterrorism literatures, and our own conjectures. They are in the nature of serious hypotheses. The result, then, is that our prototype model is intended as a serious straw man for review and debate.

Defining Factors and Values

Values and Scale

In the simplest interpretation of Figure 2.1 or other factor trees, the variables are binary: For example, there either is or is not public support; there is or is not an effective insurgent organization. The binary-variable assumption has sometimes proved useful in political science (Ragin, 1989, 2000), but a richer depiction was necessary for our purposes. The question, then, is what representation of values to use. We concluded that a discrete representation would often be natural and convenient, especially when talking with qualitatively oriented subject-matter

---

* Such observations can be inferred from the behavior of individuals who step away from terrorism—often maintaining attachment to the cause, i.e., remaining motivated even while disengaging. See especially the work of John Horgan and colleagues (Bjorgo and Horgan, 2009; Horgan, 2009).

† For primary evidence, see the Abbottabad documents captured when bin Laden was killed (Koehler-Derrick, 2012).

experts, but that the model itself should operate more continuously. Our approach, then, is as follows:

1. Allow qualitative input variables to have as many as five equally spaced discrete values, as in the set {Very Low, Low, Medium, High, Very High}. For particular contexts, allow truncated sets of permissible input values, such as {Very Low, Medium, Very High}.
2. Map qualitative values to quantitative values 1, 3, 5, 7, and 9 for the model's internal calculations, as indicated at the top of Table 2.1. If desired, input the numerical values directly. That is, express inputs in words or numbers; the model should process them as numbers in any case. When a qualitative input has a sign as well as a value (e.g., when an influence bears a negative sign), then the model retains knowledge of the "valence" and, in some calculations, treats the corresponding factors on a scale of –10 to 10, as discussed below.
3. Use stepwise-continuous mathematics within the model, operating in the interval 0 to 10 in some cases, and –10 to 10 in others, depending on whether some of the influences are negative.*
4. When outputting from the model, if discrete values are desired, round values to the nearest integer in the set {1, 3, 5, 7, 9} or the truncated set {3, 5, 7}. As appropriate, express outputs in their qualitative equivalents as shown at the bottom of Table 2.1. If continuous values are desired, as when using charts, use continuous values and maintain appropriate numerical precision to achieve smooth curves.

Table 2.1
Discretized Mapping of Qualitative and Quantitative Values of Inputs and Outputs

Qualitative Input Value for Variable X	Numerical Value Used in Model
Very Low	1
Low	3
Medium	5
High	7
Very High	9
Numerical Range for Model Variable X	**Output Value of X, if Discretized**
$0 \leq X < 2$	1, Very Low
$4 \leq X < 4$	3, Low
$6 \leq X < 8$	5, Medium
$8 \leq X < 10$	7, High
$10 \leq X < 12$	9, Very High

NOTE: If the smaller set {Low, Medium, High} is used, it is interpreted as mapping from the ranges 0–4(-), 4–6(-), and 6–10, respectively, but with representative values of 3, 5, and 7 so that the words Low, Medium, and High mean the same throughout the model.

* Inputs can be entered as any number on the continuous scale of 0 to 10, but the menu-driven model interface, described in the next section, is designed for discrete qualitative values mapped quantitatively as 1, 3, 5, 7, and 9.

We normally chose the five-scale because discussions on a three-scale {Low, Medium, High} often lead quickly to an insistence on in-between values. Our experience indicates that the desire to keep splitting differences does not persist and that five levels are typically satisfactory. That said, some displays use the three-point scale for simplicity.

The Meaning of Values

Given decisions on the scale and values, the next question is how to define the values. That is, what does Very Low or Very High mean? This is a standard problem in many social-science activities. Addressing it requires sharpening the meaning of qualitative terms for the problem domain of interest. In what follows, we first discuss the values for the top-level factor or effect, Public Support for Insurgency and Terrorism. We then discuss the values for the contributing factors.

Characterizing Public Support

We define the meanings of Very High, High, Medium, Low, and Very Low as follows:

- *Very High* represents cases in which the insurgency definitely has the considerable positive support that it needs from the public for success (e.g., resources and sanctuary) and is not significantly hampered by public opposition. The insurgency may fail for other reasons, but Public Support will not be limiting. Example: Observers report that "Serious trouble is almost surely brewing and the public supports it."
- *High* represents cases in which the insurgency has considerable positive support but has some weaknesses, such as less than full enthusiasm by supporters or the presence of significant opposition. Example: Observers report that "Serious trouble may well be brewing, although there are at least some counter currents within the public."
- *Medium* represents cases in which the insurgency has significant positive support, but the support is either not sufficiently strong to provide all that the insurgents need, or the positive support is balanced by opposition. Example: Observers report that "It is hard to characterize the situation: There are conflicting currents and counter currents; it is not evident as yet that trouble is brewing, but the ingredients are there."
- *Low* represents cases in which there is little positive support for the insurgency or in which any such support is more than offset by opposition. Example: Observers report that "While there is significant support from elements of the public, the bulk of the public is neutral or opposed, with those opposed holding more sway."
- *Very Low* represents cases in which there is little or no positive support for the insurgency or some support, but with much greater opposition. Example: Observers report that "The insurgent cause has no resonance with the public generally; although there may be pockets of supporters, the broader public ranges from neutral (or apathetic) to oppositional and would likely help authorities in maintaining law and order."

These values are intended conceptually not as ordinal numbers, but rather as "equally spaced" values.

Characterizing the Factors Contributing to Public Support

We use the same scale for the factors organizational effectiveness, motivation, perceived legitimacy of violence, and acceptability of costs and risks. However, the meanings are more subtle and must, in a sense, be "on the same scale" in terms of potential effect. Someone characterizing these factors should judge the extent to which a factor is strong enough to do "its part" in establishing full public support for an insurgency and terrorism. For example, if the insurgent organization is well led and managed, it should be assigned a High or Very High value independent of the other factors. Even if the insurgency's cause simply does not resonate with the population, organizational effectiveness is still High or Very High. Conversely, if the factors motivation, perceived legitimacy of violence, and acceptability of costs and risks are all Very High, and organizational effectiveness—although strong—is contributing only marginally on top of those other factors, its value should still be High or Very High.

Table 2.2 illustrates the kind of form one might use in asking experts to characterize the factors for a particular situation. In this case, the characterization is that the insurgent organization has low effectiveness, that public motivation is mixed or of only moderate intensity, that those who support the insurgency tend to see violence (even terrorist violence) as legitimate, although not strongly so, and that the public as a whole sees high risks in providing support and is therefore not very willing to do so. Appendix C discusses subtleties of expert elicitation in more detail.

The Issue of Probabilities

We have not associated the levels with "probabilities," but some experts may find probabilistic language useful for distinguishing levels.* Thus, a motivation value of Very High would mean that it is very likely (80–100 percent) that motivation is high enough to trigger insurgency if the other factors are not limiting (e.g., have at least Medium values). Such an approach can be heuristically valuable, but the "probabilities" should be understood as relative, contingent, and probably correlated.

Before proceeding, we should also mention briefly that the nature of public support is itself a complex issue. For example, support may be active (e.g., providing save havens or resources) or passive (e.g., turning a blind eye to insurgent activities). A richer discussion of this can be found in earlier materials (Paul, 2009; Davis et al., 2012).

Measurement on a Common Scale

As mentioned above, we used a 0 to 10 scale for measuring the inputs and outputs of this model, although retaining knowledge of whether an influence is positive or negative. Inside the model, most calculations use that knowledge of sign and make use of a –10 to 10 scale. The mapping of higher-level outputs to a 0 to 10 scale is convenient, but means that low numbers

Table 2.2
An Illustrative Characterization of Factors for a Specific Context

Value	Very Low	Low	Medium	High	Very High
Organizational Effectiveness	☐	☒	☐	☐	☐
Motivation	☐	☐	☒	☐	☐
Legitimacy of Violence	☐	☐	☒	☐	☐
Acceptability of Costs	☐	☒	☐	☐	☐

* The probabilistic interpretation is built in to approaches that use Bayesian nets or influence nets using tools such as Netica (Norsys Corporation) or GeNIe/SMILE (see University of Pittsburgh, no date).

correspond to some combination of noninterest and antipathy to the insurgency and/or its violence. Figure 2.2 shows the mapping graphically. A large negative influence, such as extreme antipathy or complete apathy/noninterest, would both be mapped on to the zero of the 0 to 10 scale.*

Mathematics of Combining Relationships

As indicated in Table 1.1, a major challenge was to identify a modest set of mathematical functions to represent the ways that factors combine. The challenge is not about expressing statistical correlations, but rather about expressing interactions among causal factors at a given time and location. *A priori*, it was not evident that we could find useful mathematical representations. When modelers attempt to reflect such information in computer programs, they often assume implicitly that a simple averaging will be meaningful, but that is surely misleading in many cases. We sought to do better.

The following paragraphs describe our effort to identify a first minimum set of necessary mathematical forms. We considered many other possibilities and variants along the way.

Approximate "And" Relationships

Figure 2.1's top-level factors are connected by "~ands," indicating that public support for insurgency and terrorism requires that, to a first approximation, all of those factors are present. The mathematics can be represented as follows in terms that assume familiarity with vectors and arrays in which a scalar, inner, or dot product is the sum of the products of the vector components and their weights (i.e., a kind of average).

If n factors combine at a node N, we can form a factor vector $\mathbf{F}^0$ with n components. We can also define a threshold vector $\mathbf{T}$ with its values being the thresholds of each component of $\mathbf{F}^0$. It follows that $\mathbf{F}^0 - \mathbf{T}$ is a vector of comparisons of each component with its threshold. We

Figure 2.2
Mapping from a Symmetric to One-Sided Scale

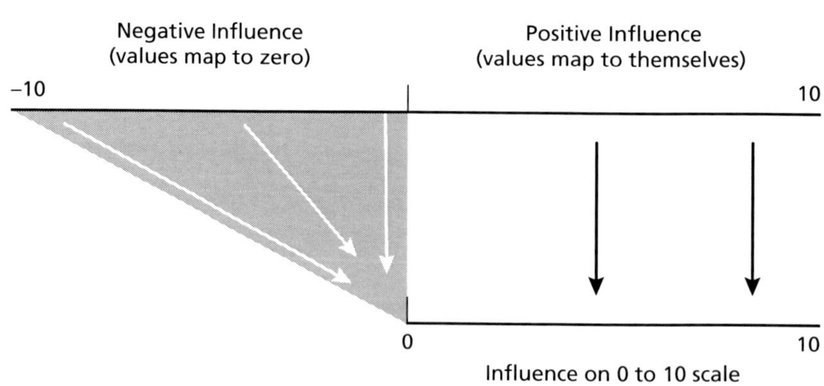

RAND *TR1220-2.2*

* Similar mapping occurs in such other domains as political campaign polling, which may be summarized by percentage of the public favoring a candidate. The percentage that does not favor the candidate includes those who loathe the candidate and those who just find the candidate weaker than another. Prior to such summarizing, however, details must be retained because the operations of combining factors and mapping to the simplified scale do not commute mathematically.

then refer to **F** as the "thresholded vector" and define it by requiring that its components are either the same as those of $\mathbf{F}^0$, or zero, depending on whether or not the component reached its threshold. If the original vector has associated weights $\mathbf{W}^0$, the weights of the thresholded vector need to be renormalized so that they will still add up to 1.

Table 2.3 describes this in mathematical terms, with explanations in the right column.

The precise expression in a particular programming language will be unique to that language. For example, the program might use If-Then-Else, For, or While loops. The mathematical expression in Table 2.3 is much better for expressing the concepts sharply and in a language-independent manner.

The thresholds for the various factors can be different, and can be either small or large, providing a great deal of flexibility. For example, by setting the thresholds to Very Low levels, the formulation reduces to linear weighted sums. Also, if there is skepticism about the absolute necessity of a given factor (recall the "~" in the "~ands" of Figure 2.1), then its threshold may be set lower than those of the others.*

Table 2.3
Mathematical Expression of "And" Relationships

Expression	Explanation
$\mathbf{F}^0 = \{F_1^0,\ldots F_n^0\};\ \mathbf{W}^0 = \{W_1^0,\ldots W_n^0\}$	Vectors of original factors and weights
$\mathbf{F} = \{F_1,\ldots F_n\};\ \mathbf{W} = \{W_1,\ldots W_n\}$	Thresholded vectors and renormalized weights
$\mathbf{F} = Max(\mathbf{F}^0 - \mathbf{T}, 0)$	A given component of the thresholded vector is 0 if the original component failed to reach its threshold, but equals the original value otherwise[a]
$\mathbf{W}^0 * \mathbf{F} \equiv \{W_1^0 F_1,\ldots W_n^0 F_n\}$	The vector of weighted scores: products of the original weights and the thresholded vector components
$\mathbf{W} = \dfrac{\mathbf{W}^0 * \mathbf{F}}{\sum W_j^0}$ $j \in \{\text{set with } \mathbf{F} \neq 0\}$	The vector of renormalized weights has components that are 0 or, for components with nonzero *F* values, are the original weights divided by the sum of original weights
$N = \mathbf{W} \bullet \mathbf{F} = \sum_i W_i F_i$	The node's value (i.e., the effect of the contributing factors) is the scalar (dot) product of the thresholded vector and the renormalized vector of weights.

[a] This assumes positive components. The generalization is given in Appendix D.

* Another way to reflect the approximate nature of the relationship would be to add a random-error term to equations. Instead, we assess the "confidence" in results estimated with the basic equations. That is discussed in a later subsection.

Representing "Or" Relationships

Distinct Cases

The cryptic use of "ors" in factor-tree depictions (which might better be written as "~ors") highlights the fact that the factors in question are not all required for the node into which they feed to have a significant value, i.e., for the effect in question to be strong. Further, they may substitute for each other. The "ors" represent ambiguous information, however, and quite a number of distinct combining relationships are possible. We found it necessary to distinguish the following cases:

1. *Any one will do.* Sometimes, only the largest factor matters. Motivation, for example, may stem from any of a number of causes. In a given context, any one of them may suffice with the others (or their absence) being irrelevant.
2. *Any one or a combination will do.* A factor's value may be high because one or a combination of subfactors combine to achieve sufficient effect. To use the example of motivation again, some people in a group may have one basis for motivation, and some another, but with the result that, overall, the group is significantly motivated. For in-between cases, an effect may be achieved primarily with one factor, but with some incremental reinforcement by others (but not dilution).
3. *Multiple factors matter and may either reinforce, counter, or dilute.* Some factors have a mix of subfactors with positive and negative influences. The positive subfactors can combine to reinforce the effect, but the negative subfactors can counter the effect, and factors with low values can dilute it. The net effect may be in between (akin to averaging) or it may be that the largest factor trumps the others.
4. *Multiple thresholded factors matter and may reinforce, counter, or dilute.* This is the same as (3), except that only factors reaching threshold values of significance matter. This kind of "thresholded linear weighted sum" is quite different than that for the "~and" combination. For values of a factor less than its threshold, the function is evaluated as 0 (or, in a variant, as the factor's threshold value).

Appendix D discusses these issues in much more detail, with both simple examples and generalizations.

These combining relations can be related to normal-life social situations: If "no one cares very much," then behavior of a group may reflect a kind of tacit compromise among weak preferences. If someone powerful cares strongly, then the group's behavior may simply reflect that preference. In this case, the rest of the group's lack of preference is not a "negative" acting against the strong preference. If there are strong opposing preferences, however, then one preference may prevail or the result may be a compromise. What description is apt depends on the particular groups and time. That is, the appropriate mathematical form depends on the circumstances; it is an empirical matter, not a matter of mathematics alone. This implies that we must reflect this uncertainty in the model itself.

> The appropriateness of our hypothesized functional forms should be assessed by experiments in social psychology and political science, and applied contextually.

Table 2.4
Alternative Models for Combining with "Ors"

Case	Description	Comment
1. Any one will do	$N = F^*$, where $F^* W^{(1)} = \text{Argmax}[\mathbf{W}^* \text{Abs}(\mathbf{F})]$	The node's value *N* is the value of the contributing factor with the largest weighted absolute value.
2. Any one or a combination will do	*P* and *S*: primary and secondary factors Four cases, with N being node value on 0 to 10 scale	*P* and *S* are the signed factor values for those factors with the largest and second-largest weighted absolute scores
	1. $P \geq 0$ and $S \geq 0$: If $S \leq \frac{10}{RW}$ Then $N = P + MR\frac{S}{10}$ Else $N = P + M$	*P* and *S* are both positive; the adjustment adds, with *M* being the maximum value of the adjustment. Here and below, *M* is positive or 0.
	2. $P \geq 0$ and $S < 0$: If $S \geq \frac{10}{R}$ Then $N = P + MR\frac{S}{10}$ Else $P - M$	*P* is positive or zero; *S* is negative; the adjustment subtracts because *S* is negative. The result is no smaller than *P* – *M*.
	3. $P < 0$ and $S \geq 0$: If $S \leq \frac{10}{R}$ Then $N = P + MR\frac{S}{10}$ Else $N = P + M$	*P* and *S* are positive and negative, respectively. The adjustment adds; The result is no more than *P* + *M*.
	4. $P < 0$ and $S < 0$: If $S > \frac{10}{R}$ Then $N = P + MR\frac{S}{10}$ Else $P - M$	*P* and *S* are both negative; the adjustment subtracts but the result is no less (no more negative) than – Abs(*P*) – *M*.
3. Net effect	$N = W \bullet F = \sum_i W_i F_i'$	The net effect is an "average" (a weighted sum of signed factors). It may be positive or negative.
4. Thresholded net effect	$N = \sum_i W_i F_i'$, where in one variant, $F_i' = Max(F_i^0, F_i)$ and, in another variant, $F_i' = 0$ if $\lvert F_i \rvert < \lvert F_i^0 \rvert$	The result is as in Case 3 except that component values are replaced in the sum by 0 or their threshold values if the components are below thresholds. See Appendix D for details.

NOTE: Results are on a –10 to 10 scale and must subsequently be mapped onto the interval 0 to 10, and then to the range 0 to 9, for consistency with inputs being limited to the set {1,3,3,7,9}.

Mathematics for the Four Cases

The four cases discussed above can be treated with the equations in Table 2.4. They include the concept of the factors having weights, as discussed more fully in later paragraphs. For now, let us focus on relating the equations of Table 2.4 to the cases above. Our formulation for Case 2 uses an approximation in which only the largest two weighted factors matter, with the others being ignored. This could be readily generalized. The two factors must be properly signed. That is, if the convention is to provide all inputs as positive numbers (but noting which are positive and which are negative influences), then, when constructing the factor vector, the negative signs must be inserted explicitly.

The equations in Table 2.4 generate results on the scale from –10 to 10. They must later be mapped onto the 0 to 10 scale indicated in Table 2.1 (all negative scores become 0's) and, for the purposes of this report, further constrained to be in the interval 1 to 9 to be consistent with constraints on inputs.*

Mathematics for the "Primary Factors Methodology"

Case 2 of Table 2.4 corresponds to what we call the "Primary Factors methodology." Actually computing the results is more complex than it might appear, and the code for doing so will look different depending on the programming language. The mathematics, however, is straightforward, as indicated in Figure 2.3. The first step is to aggregate any ambiguous (+/–) influences for which that is appropriate, as discussed in the next section, and to then construct the appropriate signed vector of factors (i.e., a factor having negative effects in a factor tree will have a negative sign). The next step is to apply a sorting operator. The sorting is based on the absolute values of the factor vector, not their signed values. Next, a slicing operator can identify the primary and secondary factors (by name), after which a selection operator can select the appropriate signed values from the original factor vector. The next step is to compute the score, which—as described in Table 2.4—is the primary factor plus an adjustment reflecting some influence from the secondary factor. All of this mathematics depends on using signed values of the influences. The last step is to map results onto the one-sided scale 0 to 10, as described in Table 2.1, and to constrain results to the range 1 to 9 so as to avoid problems due to inputs being restricted to the set {1,3,5,7,9}.

Figure 2.3
Schematic of Mathematics for Primary Factors Calculation

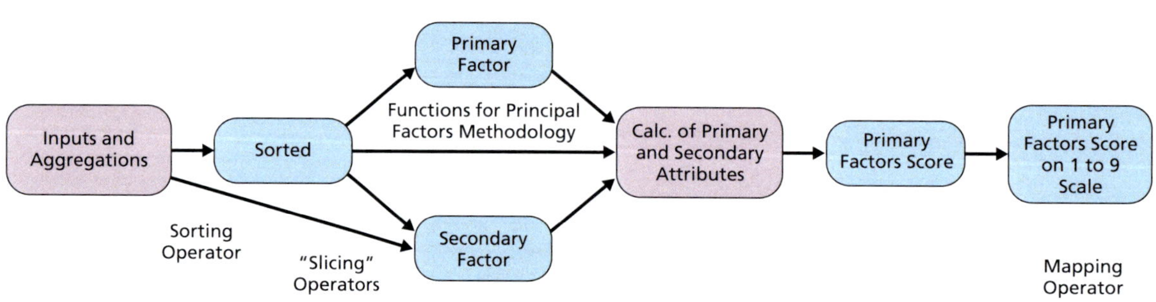

RAND *TR1220-2.3*

* These equations are numerical approximations that behave properly. Their form is motivated by a fuller treatment of the algebra.

Representing Intensity and Weight of Influence

Factor trees sometimes indicate that some factors are more important than others, as illustrated in Figure 2.4 for the case of al Qaeda (Davis et al., 2012). What should this correspond to mathematically? It might seem obvious that this simply corresponds to "weighting factors." However, the issue is not so simple. It is sometimes necessary to distinguish between the intensity of the influence and its weight. A factor tree that indicates with line width a rough sense of relative significance is implicitly conflating intensities and weights. In specifying a model, disentangling weights and intensities may be necessary. Some examples may help to explain this. Suppose that two influences, A and B, affect a node, C. If we ask about the score, strength, or intensity of A and B in isolation, as in "How important is religion to this population of people?" or "How much does this population identify with such-and-such a group?" we might be told that both A and B should be scored as 10's. However, in the context of the two factors combining to determine the value of C, one of the factors may be more salient than the other. For example, strong life-long friendships proved less salient than identity in determining how people behaved in the Balkans during the 1990s. It is not that the previous friendships were weaker in an absolute sense than they had been before, but they had less weight than identity in deciding which side to be on when side-taking became necessary for survival.

As a second example, consider two factors affecting the political position of an elected representative. Suppose that the person was a devout Catholic who strongly opposed abortion (a religious factor) but was also a believer in the separation of church and state (a political factor). When voting on a proposed bill, the representative might conclude that religious views were not salient to the decision; or, conversely, that religious conscience trumped political theory. Both factors would be strongly felt, but their relative weights would depend on the person and specific issue. Identity, then, is a multidimensional concept.

Figure 2.4
Illustrative Factor Tree Indicating Relative Strengths

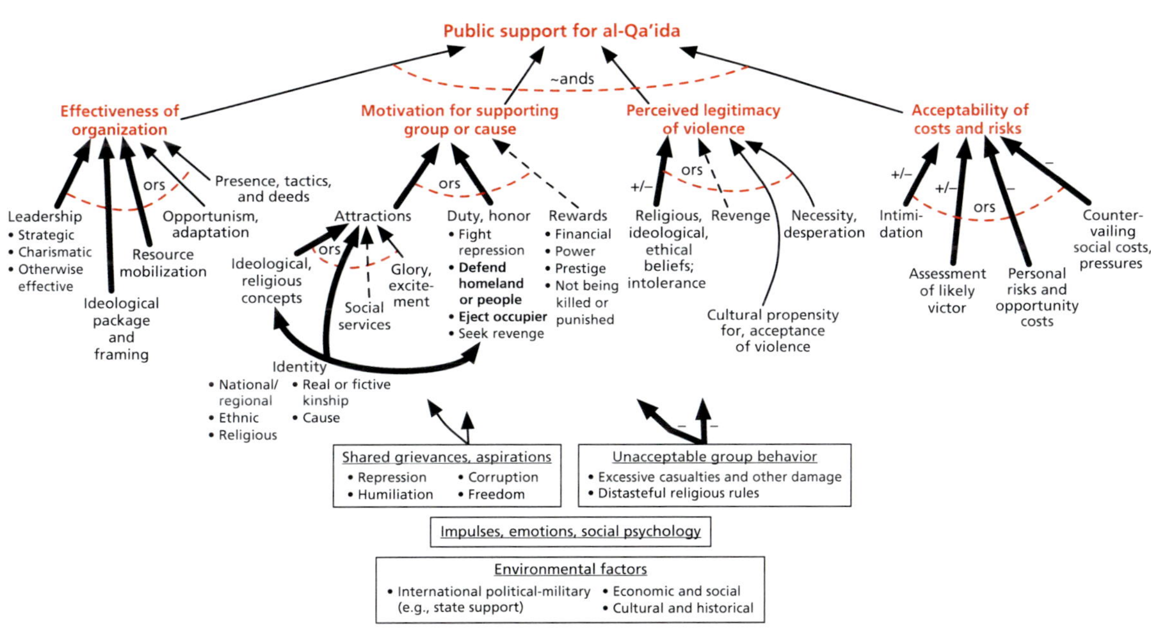

NOTES: Applies at a snapshot in time. Current factor values can affect future values of some or all other factors.
RAND *TR1220-2.4*

In summary, when translating a factor tree's arrow thickness into model constructs, we should keep both intensity and weight in mind. This is illustrated in the next section.

Resolving Ambiguous Influences

A special problem arises when dealing with influences marked +/– on a factor tree. This may mean (1) randomness or uncertainty or (2) unresolved conflicting influences.

Randomness and Uncertainty

It may be that the influence is appropriately identified but not its direction. For example, we might know that a particular faction in the population has great influence, dictated by its leader, but not know which direction the leader is leaning. To make things worse, the leader might be ambivalent and change positions from time to time based on matters not visible to us from the outside, such as personal disputes. In the first case, the factor would be deterministic, but its value could be represented by a subjective probability distribution. In the second case, the factor would effectively be driven by a random process. It could again be represented by a probability distribution, but it might be necessary to "roll the dice" each time the model was applied to a different snapshot in time. Thus, care must be taken in using probabilistic models, including Monte Carlo machinery.

> "Using Monte Carlo methods" means little without knowing what kinds of uncertainties are being treated, and how.

Unresolved Conflicting Influences

If the ambiguity arises because the population is heterogeneous, with different factions having opposite influences (e.g., favoring or opposing an action), then the ambiguity should sometimes be resolved by representing the influences separately. That approach, however, proliferates factors. It is often more convenient, and even appropriate, to aggregate. If so, the question becomes how to aggregate. Which situation applies: to aggregate or not to aggregate?

The primary issue is not mathematics, but what the real-world phenomenon is like. Is it as though the conflicting influences resolved themselves as a separate issue, or is it as though the conflicting influences remain independent as they combine with other influences? The answer is not visible from the factor tree itself. With no further information than the factor tree, it would be mathematically unsound to aggregate the +/– components of an influence, because that aggregation operation might not commute with subsequent elements of the calculation. However, if the actual phenomenon is as though the +/– factors resolve themselves, then the aggregation is not only permissible but appropriate. A number of possibilities suggest themselves, all of which involve two factions with opposite signs to their influence:

1. One faction will win out—even if by a small margin—and its preferences will utterly dominate.
2. Neither faction wins out, on this issue, and the factor's aggregate value is an average.
3. One faction wins out, but the factor's aggregate value is a somewhat watered-down version of the stronger faction's position.
4. Neither faction "wins out" and tensions continue: The factions' influences are best treated as separate and independent factors, not aggregated.

All of these occur in the real world of human behaviors, even within terrorist organizations where arguments occur about everything from objectives to tactics.

Thus, whether or not to deal with conflicting influences of the same type by aggregating will depend on the situation. We need a mathematical formulation that will highlight this uncertainty, as well as allowing for the cases of randomness and uncertainty described earlier. Table 2.5 summarizes our approach. Cases 1 and 2 deal with uncertainty and randomness. Cases 3 and 4 deal with unresolved faction-level influences. We use a single function, SIMD (Stronger Influence Mostly Dominates), that we developed for dealing with two influences, X_1 and X_2, with weights W_1 and $W_2 = 1 - W_1$. The equation contains a parameter, p, the value of which should be set differently depending on whether aggregate influence is the influence of stronger faction, aggregate influence is that of stronger faction but with some moderation due to disagreement, or aggregate influence is a simple weighted average of the competing faction influences). The parameters p have values 0, 1/4, and 1, respectively. We use 1/4 as the default value.

> The postulated functions should be tested by social psychologists, political scientists, and others who deal empirically with how such social conflicts are resolved.

Treatment of Cross-Cutting Factors

When constructing factor trees, influence diagrams, or other forms of graphical depictions of causality, it often happens that some of the lower-level variables or factors are cross-cutting. Identity is an important such factor in Figure 2.1. While support-for-terrorism issues are often *posed* in terms of religious or ideological differences, the underlying consideration is often iden-

Table 2.5
Mathematics for Ambiguous but Non-Random (+/–) Influences

Case	Approach
1. Single influence with stable but unknown sign	Vary sign parametrically (run model each way) or represent sign with a subjective probability distribution
2. Single influence with unstable sign (random process)	Represent sign with a subjective probability distribution, rolling dice in each new application of model
3. Competing factions with same type but oppositely signed influences, and with aggregation appropriate.	If $Abs(W_1X_1) \geq Abs((1-W_1)X_2)$ Then $X_1 + p[W_1X_1 - (1-W_1)X_2 - X_1]$ Else $-X_2 + p[W_1X_1 - (1-W_1)X_2 - X_1]$
3a. Stronger side dominates completely.	$p = 0$
3b. Stronger side wins but result reflects some moderating influence of weaker side	$p = 1/4$
3c. Resulting influence is just an average of factions' influences	$p = 1$
4. As in (3), but with aggregation inappropriate	Replace the +/– influence of the factor tree with separate and independent positive and negative influences

NOTE: Results in case 3 are initially on a –10 to 10 scale. The equation expresses aggregate score as the dominant factor plus a fraction p of the correction for "fair score," which is arguably $W_1X_1 - W_2X_2$.

tity, which affects what may be or at least seem to be ideological motivation and also a sense of duty and honor. The people involved may have little or no depth in thinking about ideology or religion, but they know to what group they belong if forced to choose sides. We did not represent identity explicitly in our prototype, leaving it to the user to reflect considerations of identity in estimating values of the several higher-level factors. It is unclear from social science that the web of related factors can be meaningfully disentangled. Going deeper into the representation of a factor is sometimes more analytically pretentious than accurate or useful.

In many other cases, it is possible to avoid cross-cutting influences by either reformulating (i.e., choosing new variables that separate causal flows) or by approximating relatively weak cross linkages with constants (eliminating the cross links). Similar issues arise in System Dynamics and efforts generally to design multiresolution models. Recognizing that approximations deep in the model are often rather accurate can greatly simplify the models, as in turning highly interconnected networks into hierarchical trees (Davis and Bigelow, 1998).

All of this said, some factors are in fact cross-cutting and need to be represented that way, as discussed in the following paragraphs (see, e.g., the factors at the bottom of Figure 2.1). Our approach is then to treat them like any of the other factors when combining them with others. Some subtleties should be noted. First, we are not double counting when recognizing influence through more than one branch of the tree. In the real world, a cross-cutting factor may indeed affect more than one of the higher-level factors (and even have some additional direct effect on the top-level factor). As a second subtlety, suppose that there were statistical-empirical evidence of the cross-cutting factor's influence on results (the value of the top-most factor). That would probably reflect its combined influence through two or more paths. Inferring from the empirical analysis what values to set for the individual factors might be difficult.

Time and Exogenous Factors

Extending and sharpening a static model is the focus of this report, but—over time—many factors affect one another indirectly. The result is complex, and, as in social phenomena generally, reliable predictions are often impossible. Unintended consequences of actions eventually occur—some positive and some negative. Nonetheless, dynamic modeling can be valuable by providing an integrated view of the whole even if predicted trajectories are highly uncertain. Also, in some instances, the trajectories are less uncertain than one might think because they are over-determined. A number of research groups are using such dynamical models as COMPOEX (Waltz, 2008), POSM (Body and Marston, 2011), timed-influence nets, and dynamic influence nets (Haider and Levis, 2008). RAND has also modeled system dynamics of terrorism-related issues (see Davis, Bankes, and Egner, 2007, for an epidemiological simulation of how extremism can be modeled by analogy to a disease).

Success when operating over time in a complex adaptive system depends on incremental actions, monitoring, and adaptation. Policymakers can take measures to enable future adaptive course corrections. Further, they can anticipate some developments to identify mitigating actions. Philosophically, the *FARness principle* is to favor strategies that are flexible, adaptive, and robust—i.e., able to accommodate to changes of mission, circumstances, and shocks (Davis, 2012b). This was relevant in a recent DoD study on ways to mitigate the potential negative side effects of "influence actions" against violent extremist organizations. For this report, it is sufficient to note briefly what might happen with a dynamical perspective. Looking at the factor tree (Figure 2.1), consider the following as examples:

- If an insurgent organization uses tactical violence (e.g., roadside improvised explosive devices or IEDs), that may be seen by the public as legitimate, and successes may increase motivation and reduce perceived risks of supporting the insurgency. At the next snapshot in time, then, public support may be systematically higher.
- If the organization directs terrorist actions, however, those may be seen as "unacceptable group behavior" (one of the lower boxes in Figure 2.1) because of civilian fatalities and negative world reaction. Such actions could reduce motivation to support the cause, undercut the perception of terrorism, remind people of the risks of blow-back, and cast doubt on the effectiveness of the organization itself. At the next snapshot in time, then, public support may be systematically lower due to changes in several factors.
- If "exogenous events" occur, such as the United States intervening in another Muslim country (a "bad" shock) or intervening effectively in a humanitarian disaster (a "good" shock), that may affect multiple factors in the model, either increasing or decreasing public support for the insurgency at the next snapshot in time. To a significant extent, the occurrence of such events is a random process, although the relative frequency of "good and bad shocks" and perceptions about them, may be affected by strategic communication—especially those coupled with important real-world actions.
- In prior work, we have represented such dynamical events for the sake of conveying a sense of possible effects of strategic actions. Doing so is easy enough, but the resulting uncertainties in prediction are large (Davis et al., 2007). Again, then, this report about PSOT is about modeling causes of public support at a snapshot in time.

Uncertainty and Confidence of Estimates

A fundamental issue in modeling social-science phenomena is how to deal analytically with uncertainty. This has been discussed for decades in systems analysis and policy analysis (Davis and Winnefeld, 1983; Morgan and Henrion, 1992; Davis, Kulick, and Egner, 2005). What follows draws heavily on RAND's work on the subject over several decades (Davis, 2012b).

Structural Versus Data Uncertainty

In many domains, there may exist a well-structured model, but with considerable data uncertainty. This would mean only modest, if any, capability to predict system behavior because of not knowing values of the models' more important input variables. Those, however, can be treated as variable parameters in analysis. This is especially useful if the uncertainties can be reasonably bounded. If not, prediction will not be feasible, but post-diction may be possible.

In still other cases, even the *form* of the model is uncertain—i.e., what factors it should contain or how they interact. This is structural uncertainty or model uncertainty. Fortunately, it is sometimes possible to reduce structural uncertainties to disagreement about which of a small number of models has the right form, or to parameterize the uncertainty, as in writing an equation such as $Y = X^a$, where the Y is the variable of interest, X is the independent variable, and a is some empirical constant. If a were 1, the equation would be linear; if it were 2, the equation would be quadratic—corresponding to very different models.

Social-science modeling involves uncertainty and structural uncertainty in abundance. As a result, we frequently need to squelch the desire to focus on reliable predictive modeling and instead encourage modeling that will be useful but more humble, and that will provide insights and rough odds on what to expect in various circumstances, but will usually justify only limited confidence in any predictions. This is the realm of exploratory analysis (Davis, 2002, 2003a; Bigelow and Davis, 2003; Davis et al., 2007).

Randomness Versus Ignorance

Except at levels where quantum phenomena appear (as with electronic noise in instruments), it can be argued that nothing is truly "random." In social science (and specifically in human psychology), however, much that happens is functionally random. This is especially true if, in a period of interest, factors with conflicting effects pop in and out at unpredictable times and in unpredictable orders. That said, other social-science phenomena are mysterious more because of our ignorance than anything random. Often, we simply do not know what an adversary values or worries about most. Often, we simply do not understand the values of "the public" in a country struggling with insurgency and even terrorism. To be sure, these shortcomings can sometimes be mitigated by additional effort. For example, the United States currently does massive amounts of polling in Afghanistan, and did so previously in Iraq. The information is frequently useful despite problems associated with accurate polling in such circumstances.

In the current study, we encountered both classes of uncertainty, as well as a subtle offshoot. Some factors may be relatively well measured at the time of an assessment, but may change quickly as the result of events. Scientifically, what matters is the value of the variable at the time of interest, but as a practical matter we may only know its value in the past (last week, last month, last year). In such cases, the variable may have little predictive value, but may be more important in diagnosis and explanation.

Normal Versus Deep Uncertainty

Roughly speaking, normal uncertainty is what we have in mind when we understand the phenomenon but expect variations because of random effects and usual levels of uncertainty. Deep uncertainty applies when we don't understand the phenomenon (e.g., structural uncertainty about how to model it); the variations are significant and we don't know the relevant probability distribution; or we understand the phenomenon, but the uncertainties in key parameters are large and essentially irresolvable (until afterward, perhaps).

Deterministic Versus Probabilistic Modeling

Against this background, how should we do uncertainty analysis in the present modeling? Many authors use subjective probability distributions based on elicitations from subject-matter experts. The methods are well developed and available in numerous desktop tools. The primary shortcomings are (1) the tendency to assume independent probabilities for processes that are correlated, (2) the loss of visibility as to causality (the result is a net distribution of outcomes reflecting the combined effects of many uncertain variable), and (3) the reduced visibility of high-leverage distinctions among cases.

An alternative is to model phenomena deterministically, but to do so with different values of the input variables. This may be simple sensitivity analysis or more ambitious exploratory analysis that varies all of the input simultaneously without giving special credence to a particular baseline case. The primary shortcomings of this approach are dimensional explosion and an inability to easily see the net effects of many competing probabilistic influences. Exploratory analysis is most feasible and valid when models can operate at different levels of resolution, or in families with models of different levels of resolution. Variable-resolution or multiresolution modeling (used synonymously here) has been used successfully in a number of applied studies.

The best approach is often a hybrid approach that includes both deterministic and probabilistic modeling. We developed our model to support a combination of methods.

Dealing with Correlations in Probabilistic Modeling

The user-friendliness of modern modeling packages has made it possible to do probabilistic modeling easily, but the real-world values of the independent variables may be probabilistically correlated. The public in a particular country, for example, might—through culture or political realities—share beliefs and emotions pushing motivation, perceived legitimacy of violence, and acceptability of costs and risks in the same direction. Representing correlations in a causal model can be complicated and fraught with uncertainties. We concluded that our approach would be to (1) prefer deterministic exploratory analysis in most cases and (2) when using probabilistic methods, to introduce correlation parametrically and crudely, with no pretense of precision. The mechanism for doing so is discussed in Chapter Three.

Confidence of Estimates

Although PSOT is set up to show how public support for insurgency and terrorism changes as one varies assumptions about the values of underlying factors, the model is not useful if one has no idea at all about what values to use. Thus, it is necessary to estimate what range of values should be considered, which amounts to assessing the confidence one has in the input assumptions.

As above, either deterministic or probabilistic methods can be used. One approach would be to elicit estimates of each factor's value and the range of values considered plausible. Eliciting that much detail would be burdensome for both subject-matter experts and analysts. Further, the quality of the information often does not justify such detail. In considering how to assess the confidence of estimates, then, we experimented with such bottom-up approaches, but concluded that it was more practical and sometimes better to use one or both of two methods starting with the top-level factors (e.g., organizational effectiveness):

1. *Deterministic.* Elicit confidence values along with factor values from subject-matter experts, asking about confidence at the top level (i.e., "What is your confidence in estimating Perceived Legitimacy of Terrorism?"). Calculate computed overall confidence as a linear weighted sum of the confidences of the top-level factors.
2. *Probabilistic.* Elicit triangular-distribution inputs on the factor values (e.g., "What are the minimum, most likely, and maximum values you would ascribe to Perceived legitimacy of terrorism?" and calculate confidence level in the assessment of public support as a weighted sum of the individual factors' confidences. However, assume crude correlations among factor values and, thus, show results as a function of a correlation parameter. Which correlations make sense will vary with context, but, as an example to use in the prototype model, assume that

> Using probabilistic methods without accounting for correlations is substantively dubious.

$$P_{\text{conf.,legit}} = (1 - C_p) P^0_{\text{conf.,legit}} + C_p P_{\text{conf.,acc\_costs}}$$

That is, assume that the probability distribution for confidence in perceived legitimacy is tied to the probability distribution for confidence in the acceptability of costs and risks, via a correlation parameter C_p.

We built these capabilities into the model discussed in Chapter Three, but we did not exercise them very much. The user of PSOT can change the details easily (by, for example, changing the parameter values of the minimum, most likely, and maximum values ascribed to a particular node's value).

Summary of Analytic Methods

The earlier paragraphs defined a number of building-block mathematical methods. Table 2.6 shows how they were used in our prototype model. The notation •••• indicates that a method was a primary method used.

In summary, we found it possible to specify the model with a modest number of mathematical functions and some uncertain parameters. We see these as *building blocks* that should be available in the model to reflect uncertainty in the underlying social science and variations in phenomena from one context to another. Our hope is that these mathematical building blocks will apply in other social-science modeling as well.

The next section elaborates on what we did in PSOT for each of the major factors.

Modeling Assumptions for the Prototype Application

We used all of the above methods for the prototype application to public support for insurgency and terrorism. Although other users might have made different choices, Table 2.7 shows

Table 2.6
Summary of Methods

Method	Ands	Ors	+/–	Overall
Threshold Linear Weighted Sums (TLWS)	••••	••••	••••	
Primary Factors (PF)		••••	••••	
Stronger Influence Mostly Dominates (SIMD)			••••	
Early aggregation			••••	
Deferred aggregation			••••	
Simple confidence estimate				••••
Probability distributions	Optional throughout			

Table 2.7
Summary of Methods Used, by Module

<table>
<tr><th>Method</th><th>Organizational Effectiveness</th><th>Motivation</th><th>Perceived Legitimacy</th><th>Acceptability of Costs</th><th>Public Support</th></tr>
<tr><td>Threshold Linear Weighted Sums (TLWS)</td><td>First choice</td><td>Second choice</td><td>Second choice</td><td>First choice</td><td>First choice</td></tr>
<tr><td>Primary Factors (PF)</td><td></td><td>First choice</td><td>First choice</td><td>Second choice</td><td></td></tr>
<tr><td>Stronger Influence Mostly Dominates (SIMD)</td><td></td><td>Yes</td><td>Yes</td><td>Yes</td><td></td></tr>
<tr><td>Early aggregation</td><td></td><td></td><td>First choice</td><td>First choice</td><td></td></tr>
<tr><td>Deferred aggregation</td><td></td><td></td><td>Second choice</td><td>Second choice</td><td></td></tr>
<tr><td>Deterministic uncertainty analysis</td><td colspan="5">First choice</td></tr>
<tr><td>Probabilistic uncertainty analysis</td><td colspan="4">Supplementary or second choice</td><td></td></tr>
</table>

the choices that we found most comfortable as baselines. For uncertainty analysis, we considered the alternatives. The following paragraphs describe our reasoning briefly.

Organizational Effectiveness

Our own view is that a good understanding does not yet exist of how the factors contributing to organizational effectiveness combine. This is true more generally than just in counterinsurgency work. There is no consensus, for example, on what makes a great chief executive officer or even how important that officer is. It does seem clear, however, that using thresholded linear weighted sums is more appropriate than the Primary Factors method.

> All of the relationships assumed could be informed by empirical social psychology and political science.

Motivation

Our model assumes that motivation may be due to any of a number of possible sources, and that any one will do, but that the largest motivation may be reinforced somewhat by a secondary source. The other possible motivations are irrelevant—they may be completely absent. Someone may support an insurgency because of, e.g., religious zeal, a sense of identity with the insurgents, or something else—with no thoughts about earthly rewards or even glory. Initially, we used the function of Case 1 in Table 2.4, but settled on Case 2 (largest factor with some possible reinforcement).

Perceived Legitimacy of Terrorism

As with motivation, we assume that perceived legitimacy may be based on any of several rationales. However, as indicated by the +/– sign on the arrow for ideological reasons in Figure 2.1, there can be influences that either increase or reduce the perception of legitimacy. Strong religious feelings, in particular, can either justify violence (as in al Qaeda's narrative) or strongly deplore it (as in the view that unnecessary violence, including suicide terrorism, are un-Islamic and wrong). Our model assumes as a baseline that the +/– ambiguity will be resolved, with the aggregate ideologically based perception of legitimacy being largely the position of the stronger faction within the portion of the public that supports the insurgency. The overall evaluation of the variable focuses on the two primary factors at work, but one of these can be a negative ideologically based influence. Thus, the model uses Case 2 in Table 2.4 with the aggregation approach to ambiguous influences in Table 2.5. It assumes that the aggregate ideological influence will be largely (but not wholly) determined by the stronger subfaction.

Acceptability of Costs and Risks

This factor is especially complex. On the one hand, any strongly perceived risk could dominate the evaluation. However, as noted in the factor tree, the result is a function of conflicting positive and negative influences, including two influences of ambiguous sign (e.g., intimidation can either enhance or decrease the acceptability of insurgency and terrorism, depending on whether the intimidation by insurgents is stronger or weaker than that of counterinsurgency forces). In our baseline version of the model, we assume that aggregate versions of the ambiguous influences can be used, but that whether Cases 1, 2, 3, or 4 of Table 2.4 applies depends on context and the strength of the factors. The user of the model will see results for alternative assumptions about how the costs and risks combine. One set of results corresponds to the strongest-influence-dominates paradigm; the other corresponds to a weighted and thresholded "balancing" of various considerations (i.e., we use both the Primary Factors and Thresholded Linear Weighted Sums models).

Public Support for Insurgency and Terrorism

Because of the factor tree's "and" condition, we assume that the top-level public-support factor is best evaluated with thresholded linear weighted sums with relatively stringent threshold values (Medium), although a case can be made for assuming lower thresholds for organizational effectiveness and perceived legitimacy of violence (because that perception might change quickly, rendering obsolete characterizations from earlier weeks or years).

CHAPTER THREE

Implementation in a High-Level Language

Although we have defined and discussed all of the primary concepts of PSOT in Chapter Two, modelers will know from experience that models change, that documentation is always incomplete or imprecise, and that it is necessary to look in the model itself to know definitively what is there and assumed as defaults.

Choosing a Language

To implement PSOT, we sought a language that would be comprehensible to researchers from diverse fields, especially social science, and that would at the same time constitute a specification model for those wishing to implement its substantive content in diverse languages and environments. The primary features that we sought were

1. visual multiresolution modeling with influence diagrams
2. strong and intuitive use of vector and array mathematics
3. appropriateness for system modeling
4. effective means for uncertainty analysis
5. user-friendliness for people other than programmers
6. self-documentation features
7. potential for moving substantive content to other modeling environment if desired.

We did not require such features useful for other purposes as discrete-event simulation, easy compatibility with agent-based modeling, inductive reasoning, or coupling with geographic information systems.

A number of languages might have proven adequate, but most have built-in points of view narrowing their applicability.* We settled on Analytica (Lumina Decision Systems), which satisfied our criteria and was familiar from past work. Analytica grew out of an effort at Carnegie Mellon University to improve the treatment of uncertainty in policy analysis (Morgan and Henrion, 1992). It is very well documented, and researchers from diverse backgrounds can pick

* System Dynamic languages such as STELLA and iThink (ISEE Systems) take a stock-and-flow perspective and emphasize feedback effects. Commonly used languages for agent-based modeling (e.g., REPAST, SEAS, and NetLogo) derive from a bottom-up theoretical view in which macroscopic behavior "emerges" from the aggregate behavior of low-level agents (Carley and Frantz, 2009). Still other languages such as Netica are intended for use in Bayesian networks. Although a number of environments exist for "multimodeling" in which models of different types co-exist and communicate, such heterogeneity and complexity was inappropriate to our purposes.

up the features most needed for our purposes in days.* A no-cost viewer, downloadable from the web, is sufficient for purposes such as reviewing someone else's model or gaining a feel for the model. Trial copies are also available.†

The Prototype Model

PSOT is relatively self-documented and is available by request to the authors. Upon opening the model, one sees the opening screen or "face plate" (Figure 3.1). Each bubble denotes a module. The Overview module includes the factor tree on which the model is based and related text about model intent. The model itself is contained in the module called Model. The Changes node is merely a convenient place to log changes (e.g., a bug fix or addition of a new feature), which is very convenient in the absence of a more formal configuration-control system.

Double-clicking the Interface brings up what appears in Figure 3.2. Inputs are on the top portion of the interface; outputs are indicated by red nodes with "Calc" (for calculate). The inputs themselves are arranged in different layers of detail. The top four rows of inputs allow the user to specify each of the top factors from menus, either with a particular value or, where "All" appears, with a list of values to be used in parametric exploration (e.g., Low, Medium, High). Optionally, some or all of the model's lower-level inputs (8–9 rows) can be specified—again as particular values or lists. The interface, then, reflects PSOT's multiresolution modeling, which allows top-down or bottom-up reasoning and greatly simplifies uncertainty analy-

Figure 3.1
The Opening Screen

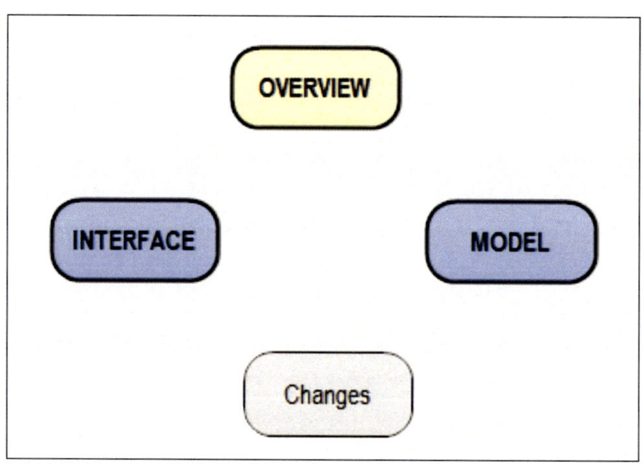

RAND *TR1220-3.1*

* One of us (Davis) uses Analytica to teach graduate-level policy analysis. Students pick up essential features in the first week. Learning Analytica's most advanced features, of course, is time-consuming and challenging, as with all languages. These features come into play with large and complex models and databases.

† The free player and a 30-day test version are available from the Lumina Decision Systems website (Lumina Decision Systems, 2012).

Figure 3.2
The Interface

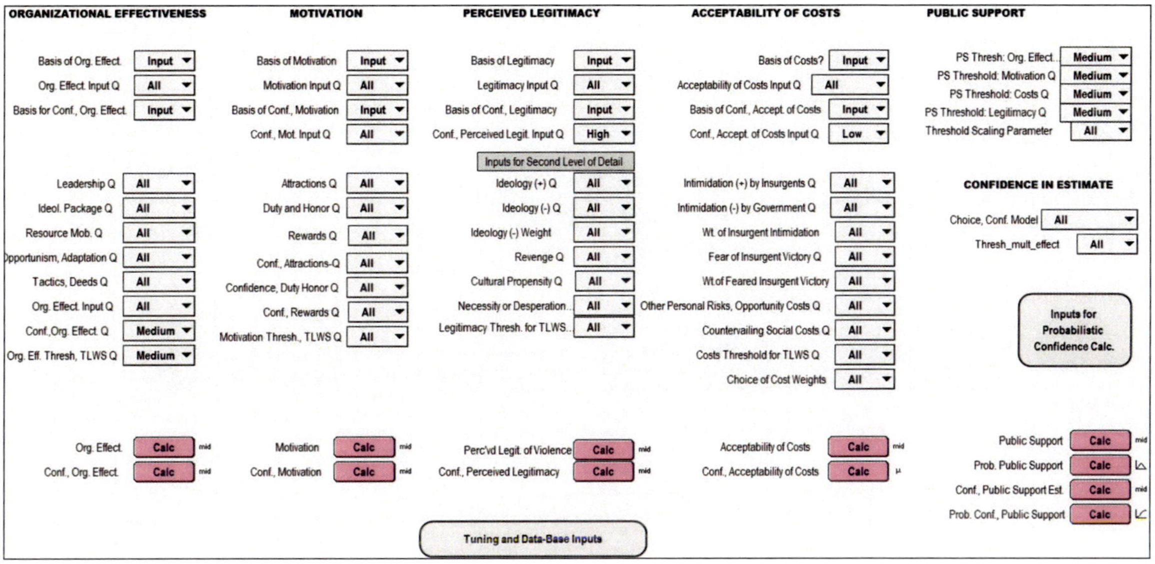

RAND *TR1220-3.2*

sis.* PSOT implements only two of the factor tree's levels of detail, but the user can add further optional detail if desired. Looking back to Figure 2.1, the cross-cutting factor of identity would be an obvious candidate for additional detail.

PSOT's structure follows the structure of the factor tree except for details that only the modeler would ordinarily look at. These relate, for example, to defining data structures, and laying out procedural flow for the program as it does various mathematical calculations and proceeds along a path depending on earlier calculations. In usual models, these features are prominent in the program itself. In PSOT, they are relegated to background in gray modules. Such gray modules may also contain nodes for verification testing, comparing results across alternative submodels, and other information useful to keep in the program as a repository.

Figure 3.3 shows the top level of the substantive model, with modules corresponding to the major elements of the factor tree. The module "Functions and Operators" (bottom) includes definitions for mathematical functions used throughout the program. These are building-block functions that could be used in analogous models, such as a model of the propensity of an individual to become an active terrorist.

Figure 3.4 shows the interior of the module for Motivation. Again, it is structured like the conceptual model it is implementing, except that it is rotated 90 degrees. We use a convention of green rectangles for inputs, red hexagons for highlighted outputs, blue shapes for other

---

* If all inputs were single values, then it might be necessary to assure that inputs made at a high level (lower resolution) were consistent with the results of making inputs at a lower level (higher resolution). We say "might" because it is not uncommon for higher-level models and data to be more accurate than lower-level (higher-resolution) models and data. In any case, consistency of models (and data) at different levels of resolution should be understood to depend fundamentally on the way in which model outputs will be used, down to the level of the question asked or whether answers to the question would change much (Davis and Bigelow, 1998). For uncertainty analysis, such complications are less important. It is instead more important that the uncertainties ascribed to higher-level factors are consistent with the result of aggregating uncertainties from lower-level factors.

Figure 3.3
The Model's Top-Level Structure

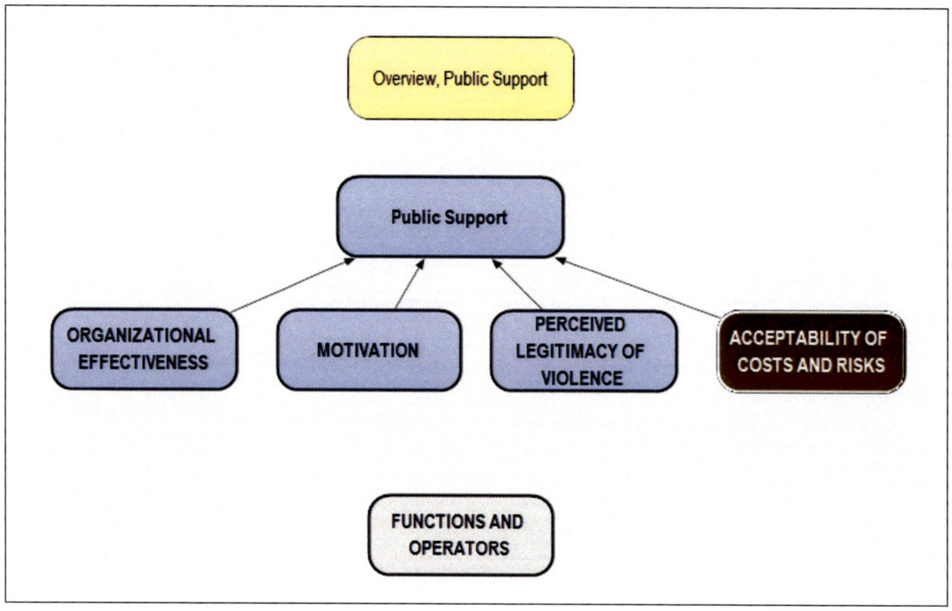

RAND *TR1220-3.3*

Figure 3.4
Structure of the Sub Model for Motivation

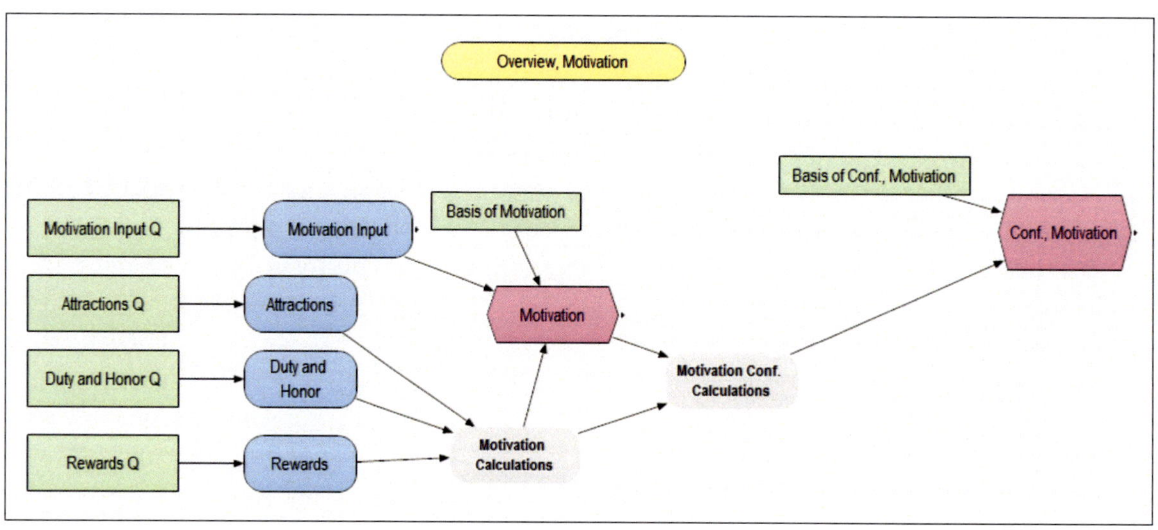

NOTE: Green rectangles indicate inputs, red hexagons indicate highlighted outputs, blue shapes indicate other variables of the model, and gray or very light shapes indicate modules (containers of nodes).
RAND *TR1220-3.4*

variables of the model, and gray or very light shapes for modules (containers of nodes). Yellow variables or modules contain documentation information.

The Q's on the input variables on the left of Figure 3.4 indicate that they are qualitative (e.g., "Low"); these are immediately transformed into quantitative variables, which in turn are inputs to the calculation of overall motivation.* The right side of the diagram estimates the confidence (Conf.) that should be ascribed to the result for motivation.

Figure 3.5 illustrates what one sees by double-clicking a given node of the model. It shows the name of the particular variable, a description (such description fields are what make it possible for the model to be relatively self-documenting), the algorithm itself (in the definition field, but without the = sign that might be expected), and a list of the inputs to this variable and the variables to which this one is outputted. In this particular case, the algorithm is Analytica-speak for a linear weighted sum, accomplished as a scalar product of two vectors (see Description for plain English).

As illustrated in this sampling of displays, a reviewer can understand the flow of what is being accomplished without seeing details of computer code. That will typically be sufficient for spotting omissions or peculiarities, or suggesting tough questions. This is much more satisfying than, say, receiving a briefing that purports to describe a model but without being able to see anything of the program itself.

Despite this relative user-friendliness, visual programming and simple syntax for elementary mathematics goes only so far. It takes a substantial amount of effort to build a program

Figure 3.5
An Illustrative Node Definition

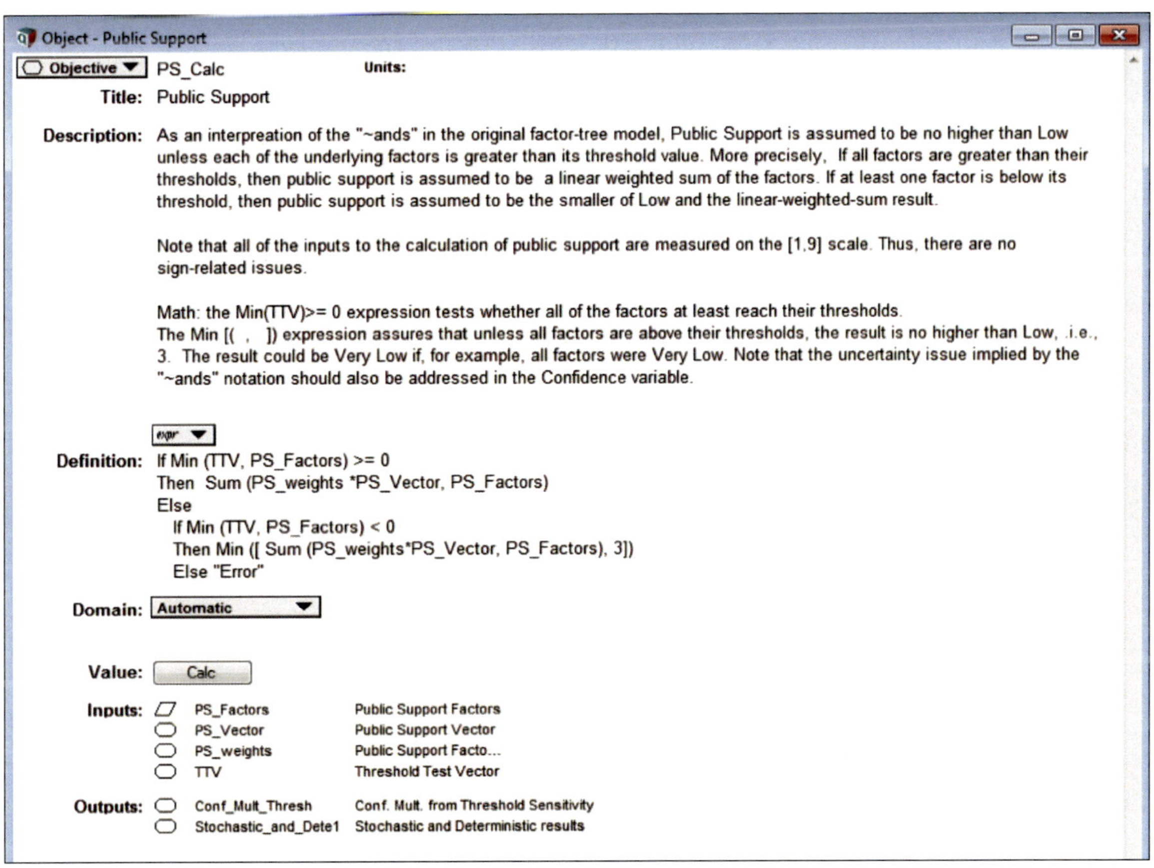

RAND *TR1220-3.5*

* Users of Analytica sometimes reserve the green rectangles for "decision variables," but we use them for all inputs that may have uncertain values.

such as PSOT. Doing so requires an appropriate technical background, and program details will not be easily understood without some programming background and knowledge of linear algebra. With such background, however, we believe the model and program are much easier to understand than if written in a language such as C, Java, or Visual Basic.

Illustrative Outputs

Figure 3.6 illustrates a simple model output assuming that the user specifies all of the top-level factors (organizational effectiveness, motivation, perceived legitimacy, and acceptability of costs and risks). Even this simplified example shows results as a function of the four inputs. It also demonstrates the nonlinearity of our thresholding assumption. Our intent was to build an uncertainty-sensitive model, and to make it relatively difficult to use the model as an answer machine. Thus, this output shows what could be called a contingent assessment. Social scientists are often criticized for answering questions with "Well, it depends." Outputs such as Figure 3.6 indicate exactly what this means.

The figure displays the contingent assessment on a 0 to 10 scale, the actual value dependent on motivation (x-axis) and acceptability of costs and risks (the bar position and color within a given group). The user can change the other variables by selecting values from the menus at the top. When the model is used live, these settings can be changed instantaneously. The output of the model can also be shown in tabular form (Table 3.1).

Figure 3.7 illustrates a probabilistic output. The particular calculation required estimating the range of possible values for each of organizational effectiveness, motivation, perceived

Figure 3.6
Parametric Assessment of Public Support

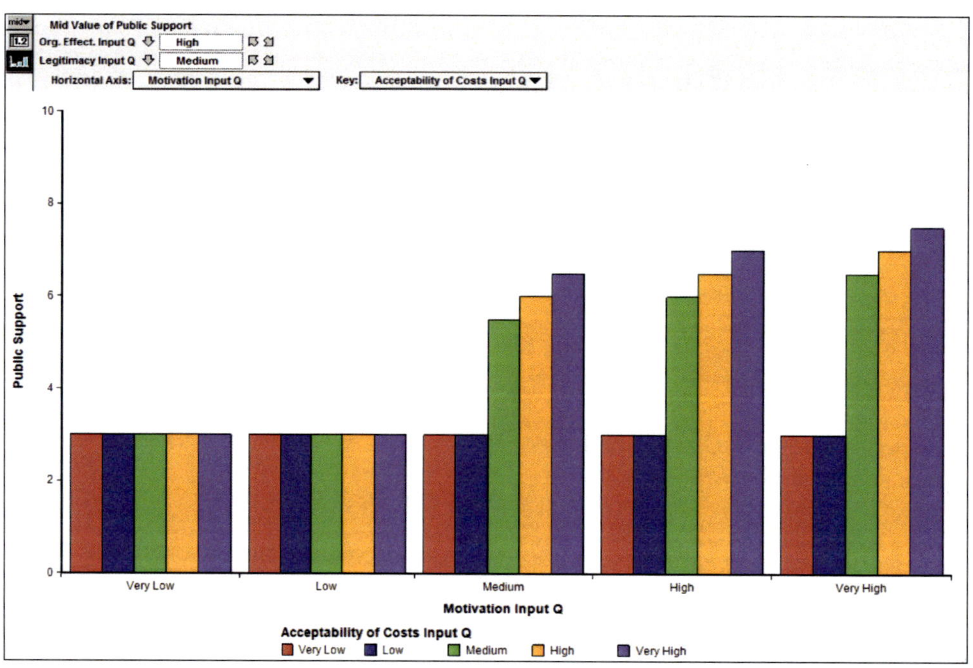

RAND *TR1220-3.6*

Table 3.1
Tabular Version of Output

Mid Value of Public Support
Org. Effect. Input Q: High
Legitimacy Input Q: Medium
Acceptability of Costs Input Q ☐ Totals
Motivation Input Q ☐ Totals

	Very Low	Low	Medium	High	Very High
Very Low	3	3	3	3	3
Low	3	3	3	3	3
Medium	3	3	5.5	6	6.5
High	3	3	6	6.5	7
Very High	3	3	6.5	7	7.5

Figure 3.7
Probability Density for Public Support

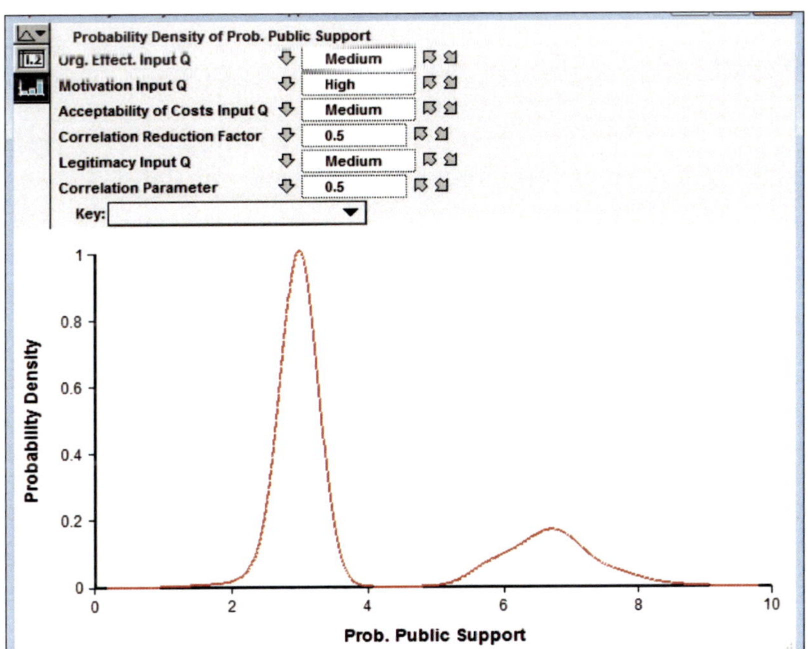

RAND *TR1220-3.7*

legitimacy, and acceptability of costs and risks (using triangular distributions). The example illustrates bimodality, something not uncommon with PSOT. Although the most likely value of public support for the assumptions made is only 3 (Low, in qualitative terms), there is a significant probability of public support being in the High range. Figure 3.8 shows the cumulative distribution function, which indicates about a 23 percent chance of a High value. These probabilities are based on a calculation assuming that the probability of the public being motivated is somewhat correlated (note the "correlation reduction parameter = 0.5", as discussed

Figure 3.8
Cumulative Probability for Public Support

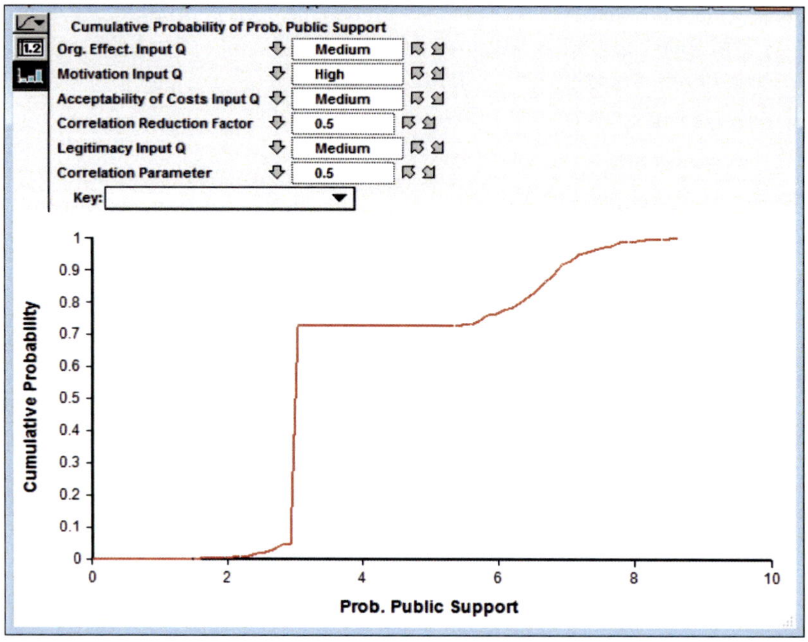

RAND *TR1220-3.8*

earlier with the probability of it seeing legitimacy and of tending to downplay costs and risks. Were we to make the common assumption of independent probabilities, the probability of a High value would drop to 10 percent.

We show additional and more complex outputs in Chapter Four when discussing exploratory analysis, but these examples give a sense of the model's outputs when the model is used at the highest level.

Model Performance

We designed PSOT for exploratory analysis with a personal computer. For many purposes, run time is instantaneous or a matter of seconds. In other cases, it may take tens of seconds to run the many cases of an exploration, but the results are then stored and the result of changing input values is essentially instantaneous change of the display.

This said, by varying enough inputs across enough values, or by doing probabilistic calculations with hundreds of samples, it is certainly possible to bring PSOT to a halt—or, more accurately—to run up against memory limitations of Windows or certain limits of Analytica. The best procedure is to exploit the multiresolution features of PSOT: exploring at the top level initially and then delving into the details on a factor-by-factor basis rather than running the model with all of the lowest-level factors inputted with multiple possible values. It is also unnecessary to use five values for each and every factor. Exploring over 10,000 runs bothers a modern laptop not at all. This could correspond, for example, to varying four factors with five values each and four inputs with two values each. We prefer running all cases (the full factorial design) because it produces easily interpretable outputs, but the obvious alternative—even for deterministic analysis—is to establish an experimental design and use Monte Carlo methods to sample the possibility space.

CHAPTER FOUR

Looking Ahead to Exploratory Analysis Under Uncertainty

Resources did not permit significant analysis in our prototype effort, but we developed PSOT in part to support exploratory analyses under uncertainty. In what follows, we illustrate exploratory analysis—first at the top level (inputting the top four factors directly) and then for a deeper look at how one of the top-level factors itself depends on lower-level factors.

Top-Level Exploration

To illustrate, Figure 4.1 shows results for Acceptability of Costs as a function of personal risks seen by the public (x-axis), the countervailing pressures in society against public support (e.g., pressures from friends, family, and tribes, as indicated by the colored bars), and other factors shown at the top left. The top pane, Figure 4.1a, is based on the Primary Factors method discussed in Chapter Two; the lower pane, Figure 4.1b, is based on Thresholded Linear Weighted Sums method. Taken together, the figures explore the variation of assessment as a function of two uncertain factors and one structural parameter (which algorithm or method to use in combining the factors). When using the model interactively, the exploration could extend to the additional variables at the top left. Note that one of the independent parameters is the relative weight (relative importance) of feared insurgent victory. Since the public is presumably concerned that it will be on the "wrong side," it will consider the possibility and consequences of either the insurgents or the government winning. A value of 0.5 for the weight in Figure 4.1 means that both fears are equally strong.

Looking more closely at Figure 4.1a, we see that, on the left side, Public Support is Very High—primarily because the insurgents are seriously intimidating the public, which has the affect of increasing the acceptability of supporting them. However, as countervailing social costs increase (e.g., resistance from family and friends), it becomes less acceptable to support the insurgents, despite the intimidation. If, in addition, there are tangible personal risks and opportunity costs (e.g., if supporting terrorists ruled out opportunities for government aid), then acceptability of support falls even more. Although intimidation by insurgents is Very High, the government forces are also exerting pressure, so the net effect of intimidation is less important (in the Primary Factors method) than personal risks and countervailing costs. In contrast, Figure 4.1b shows results using Thresholded Linear Weighted Sums. In this instance, the net effect of all influences is such that the acceptability of costs and risks is never less than medium. We selected this case to illustrate that results depend not just on the factors and their values, but on the way in which we assume that they combine. As it happens, we suspect that Primary Factors method is more accurate in describing motivation, but that is a hypothesis

Figure 4.1
Exploratory Analysis of Acceptability of Costs and Risks

a. Results using the Primary Methods Method

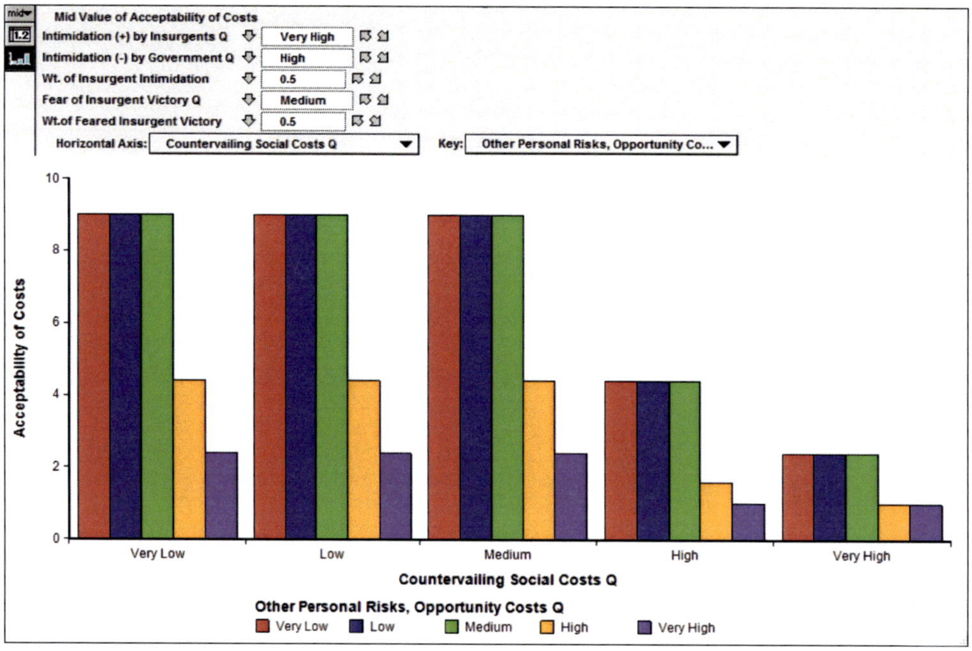

b. Results using Thresholded Linear Weighted Sums

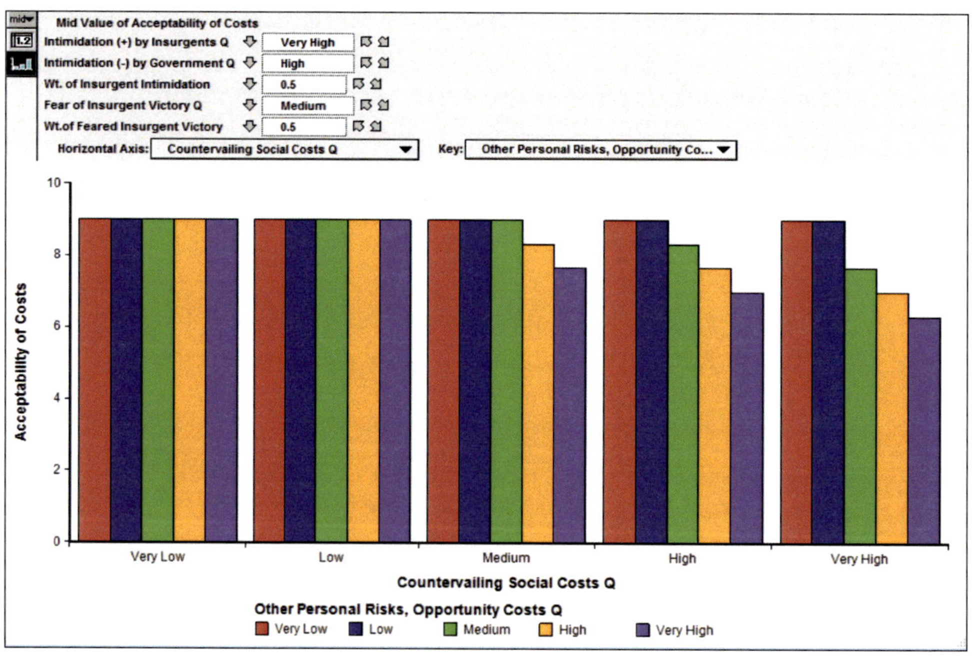

NOTE: The suffix Q indicates a qualitative value, such as "Very Low."

RAND *TR1220-4.1*

that should be examined empirically, both in social-psychology laboratories and the field. The results will probably depend on the situation.

Figure 4.2 illustrates exploration with lower-level variables of the factor tree. In this case, the inputs are the values of Organizational Effectiveness, Motivation, and Perceived Legitimacy, and the lower-level factors contributing to Acceptability of Costs. As discussed earlier, when working with such a model interactively, all of the variables shown at the top can be varied (for a total of 14)—allowing the analyst to quickly determine (tens of minutes) the combinations of assumptions that lead to good, bad, or ambiguous results. Computer search

Figure 4.2
Exploration with Detail for Acceptability of Costs

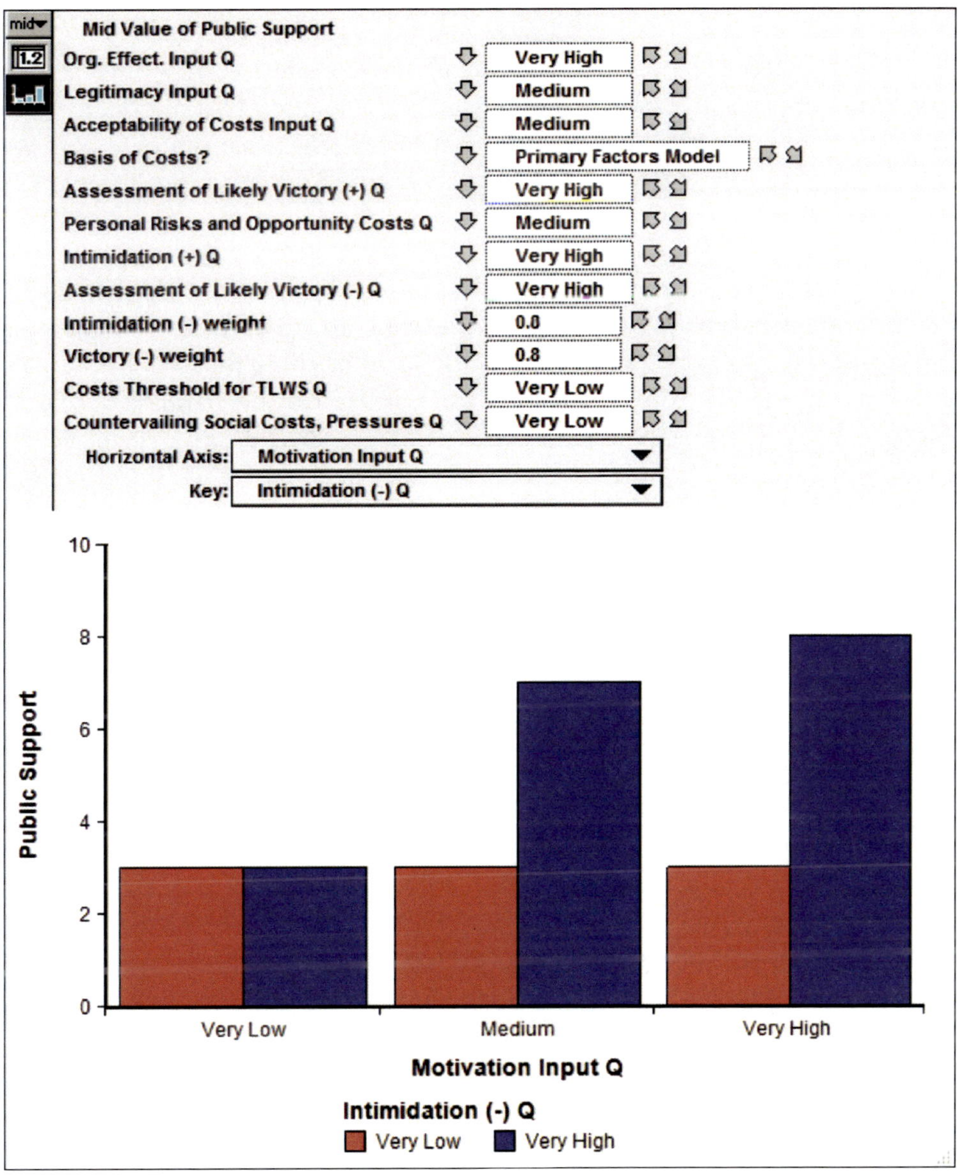

NOTE: Reference to intimidation is to aggregate intimidation, as discussed in Chapter Two. Thus, it is the net result of intimidation by both insurgents and government.

RAND *TR1220-4.2*

methods can also be used, with techniques such as data mining, some of which are becoming quite sophisticated and can automatically find the various interesting regions of the assumptions space.* Much can be done visually, however, so long as the model has been designed with multiple optional levels of resolution at which to operate. The most effective approach is to explore at the top level, identify which high-level factors are most important, and then increase the resolution on those, seeing the factors that underlie them. Exploration over the 14 variables involved tens of thousands of cases, completed in about 140 seconds on a desktop Macintosh. Such numbers are almost irrelevant, however, because computers are fast and uncomplaining; with an appropriate experimental design and sequenced operations, millions of runs can be made and stored in databases for visual exploration. What matters is whether the experimental design provides enough coverage to allow seeing the large view of how assumptions interact and how they matter. It is especially important that:

- If the model has been designed for multiple levels of resolution, it is possible to generate low-resolution displays that show essentially all of the low-resolution input assumptions at work, rather than having to take on faith that many other assumptions (perhaps dozens of others) are so well known as to be fixed and hidden. To an analyst, that is a powerful methodology.

The key, of course, is to synthesize the results of such explorations, whether accomplished manually or by computer processing. Much can be done to condense the insights. Table 4.1 summarizes top-level exploratory analysis in tabular form by showing PSOT results for Public Support as a function of the four top-level factors and a tuning parameter, the threshold assumed for legitimacy. The threshold parameter is Low and Medium for the upper and lower pane of Table 4.1. Table 4.1 highlights the interesting "regions" of assumptions space with color:† Red is very bad, orange is bad, yellow is marginal, light green is good, green is very good.

Deeper Exploration

Given a top-level understanding of how PSOT predicts public support, it is then important to delve deeper. To illustrate this for the factor of Acceptability of Costs and Risks, Figure 4.3 shows results of exploratory analysis in a graphic format rather than the tabular format illustrated in Table 4.1. Both format types have their advantages and disadvantages. Individuals have varied cognitive preferences.

In any case, Figure 4.3 shows results for five variables: intimidation by insurgents, countervailing pressures, fear of insurgent victory, intimidation by the government (counterinsurgency forces), and personal risk. It also assumes (not shown on the figure) use of the thresholded linear weighted sum, a weight of 0.5 on fear of insurgent victory (i.e., equal salience

* Exploiting computer search techniques for exploratory analysis was suggested two decades ago (Bankes, 1993) and has been realized in recent years (Lempert et al., 2006). See also Davis et al. (2007), which compared alternative methods for exploratory modeling and exploratory analysis, including visual and computer-search methods.

† PSOT does not itself generate such summary tables, but it exports the data, allowing them to be constructed in a spreadsheet program.

Table 4.1
Convergence with Tabular Summaries of Top-Level Exploratory Analysis

a. Legitimacy threshold is assumed Low

Organizational Effectiveness: Very Low

		Motivation								
		Very Low			Medium			Very High		
		Legitimacy			Legitimacy			Legitimacy		
		Very Low	Medium	Very High	Very Low	Medium	Very High	Very Low	Medium	Very High
Acceptability of Costs	Very Low	1	2	3	2	3	3	3	3	3
	Medium	2	3	3	3	3	3	3	3	3
	Very High	3	3	3	3	3	3	3	3	3

Organizational Effectiveness: Medium

		Motivation								
		Very Low			Medium			Very High		
		Legitimacy			Legitimacy			Legitimacy		
		Very Low	Medium	Very High	Very Low	Medium	Very High	Very Low	Medium	Very High
Acceptability of Costs	Very Low	2	3	3	3	3	3	3	3	3
	Medium	3	3	3	4	5	6	5	6	7
	Very High	3	3	3	5	6	7	6	7	8

Organizational Effectiveness: Very High

		Motivation								
		Very Low			Medium			Very High		
		Legitimacy			Legitimacy			Legitimacy		
		Very Low	Medium	Very High	Very Low	Medium	Very High	Very Low	Medium	Very High
Acceptability of Costs	Very Low	3	3	3	3	3	3	3	3	3
	Medium	3	3	3	5	6	7	6	7	8
	Very High	3	3	3	6	7	8	7	8	9

b. Legitimacy threshold is assumed Medium

Organizational Effectiveness: Very Low

		Motivation								
		Very Low			Medium			Very High		
		Legitimacy			Legitimacy			Legitimacy		
		Very Low	Medium	Very High	Very Low	Medium	Very High	Very Low	Medium	Very High
Acceptability of Costs	Very Low	1	2	3	2	3	3	3	3	3
	Medium	2	3	3	3	3	3	3	3	3
	Very High	3	3	3	3	3	3	3	3	3

Organizational Effectiveness: Medium

		Motivation								
		Very Low			Medium			Very High		
		Legitimacy			Legitimacy			Legitimacy		
		Very Low	Medium	Very High	Very Low	Medium	Very High	Very Low	Medium	Very High
Acceptability of Costs	Very Low	2	3	3	3	3	3	3	3	3
	Medium	3	3	3	3	5	6	3	6	7
	Very High	3	3	3	3	6	7	3	7	8

Organizational Effectiveness: Very High

		Motivation								
		Very Low			Medium			Very High		
		Legitimacy			Legitimacy			Legitimacy		
		Very Low	Medium	Very High	Very Low	Medium	Very High	Very Low	Medium	Very High
Acceptability of Costs	Very Low	3	3	3	3	3	3	3	3	3
	Medium	3	3	3	3	6	7	3	7	8
	Very High	3	3	3	3	7	8	3	8	9

Figure 4.3
Graphic Results of Exploratory Analysis for Acceptability of Costs and Risk (TLWS Method)

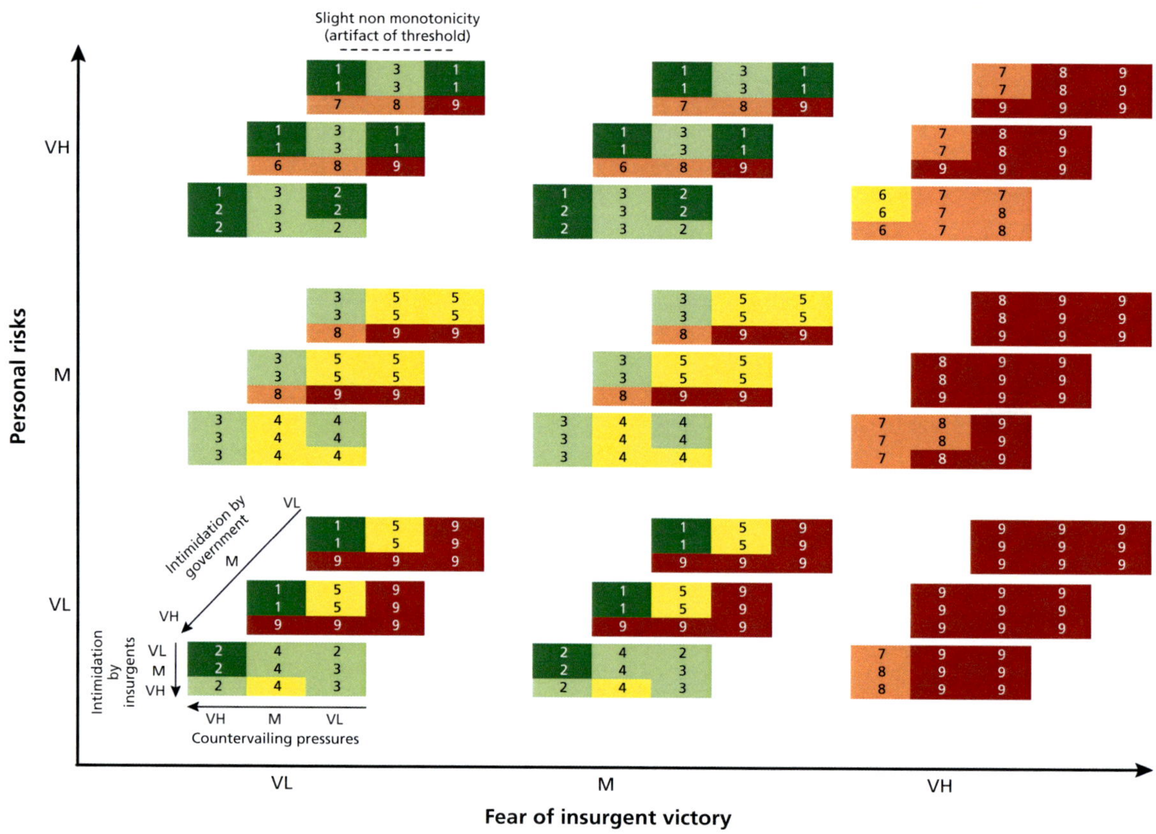

RAND *TR1220-4.3*

for fearing insurgent victory or fearing government victory), and a weight of 0.5 on weight of insurgent intimidation (i.e., equal salience for either side's intimidation).

The variables in the figure are represented along multiple axes. As one moves up figure's "main" y-axis, Personal Risks increase; as one moves horizontally across the figure's "main" x-axis, Fear of Insurgent Victory increases. One can also move along the x- and y-axes within each group of nine cells (three rows, three columns): Countervailing Pressures *decreases* moving left to right within each group of nine cells, and Intimidation by Insurgents increases moving downward within each group. Finally, one can compare the groups of cells, which in the figure are arranged in stacked sets of three nine-cell groups. Though difficult to represent on a sheet of paper, one can imagine a third dimension going "into" the paper: Intimidation by the Government *decreases* with increased depth along this dimension. (The axes for Countervailing Pressures, Intimidation by Insurgents, and Intimidation by the Government are labeled only in the lower left of Figure 4.3, but they apply throughout the figure.)

The logic for this mixture of directionalities is simple: Our intent was to sharpen the ability to see patterns by having "bad" results be preferentially toward the right, bottom, and rear, and to have "good" results be preferentially toward the left, top, and front. This determined the order in which we considered values of Very Low, Medium, and Very High.

Visual exploration quickly suggests the following:

- Acceptability of Costs will be High or Very High (red or orange) in most cases if insurgent intimidation is Very High (bottom row of each set of three rows) and fear of insurgent victory is High (right side).
- These effects are worsened if there is no government intimidation (into the page) or no personal risks (lower on page).
- Looking to the positive, public support will be Low or Very Low in most cases if members of the public perceive high personal risk in such support (top of page) or feel strong countervailing pressures against support (left side of any given triplet); and if they do not fear insurgent victory (left of page).
- This effect is strengthened if, in addition, the government intimidation is strong (the lowest nine-cell group in each stacked set of three; or, the one "closest" to the reader if the sets are considered to be arranged in three dimensions).

An additional page would cover results for the Primary Factors model. A total of eight such tables would cover the entire uncertainty space. Many other methods can be used to summarize the information. Such displays are remarkable for their density of information and—with experience—their comprehensibility.*

On the Imperfections of Approximate Mathematics

Figure 4.3 flags a curiosity in the top row of the figure. A modest non-monotonicity shows up, where acceptability of costs and risks increases and then decreases as countervailing pressures increase from Very Low to Medium and then to Very High. As the expression goes, the "behavior is a feature not a bug." That is, it is not an error in programming, but rather an artifact of the Thresholded Linear Weighted Sums method, which uses a heuristic (a simple threshold) to determine whether a given factor is or is not considered when calculating the effect. The heuristic is good most of the time, imperfect in certain cases, but never seriously wrong. The errors are small, but remind us that using approximations such as discrete factor values and thresholds can generate some odd microscopic behavior. We prefer the Primary Factors method for this calculation because it seems to us more realistic and largely avoids such problems. Appendix D discusses the assumptions and circumstances under which non-monotonic results arise. They can be avoided with a variant method.

Figure 4.4, then, shows results for the Primary Factors model, otherwise using the same assumptions and parametric as in Figure 4.3. Here the results are much more encouraging:

- The Acceptability of Costs (for supporting the insurgency and terrorism) is often high or bad (orange or red) when the fear of insurgent victory is high (right). Because the public fears insurgent victory, it accepts the costs of supporting the insurgency.
- This tendency can be offset, to greater or lesser degree by countervailing pressures, high personal risks, or government intimidation. At the top right, for example, results are much better from the counterinsurgency perspective.

---

* This display was created by manipulating data in Excel, but elegant depictions can be generated automatically with specialized display software. At RAND, such displays were first developed by Steven Bankes and James Gillogly for exploratory analysis, as illustrated in a 1994 compendium (Davis, 1994).

Figure 4.4
Graphical Results for Acceptability of Costs and Risks (Primary Factors Method)

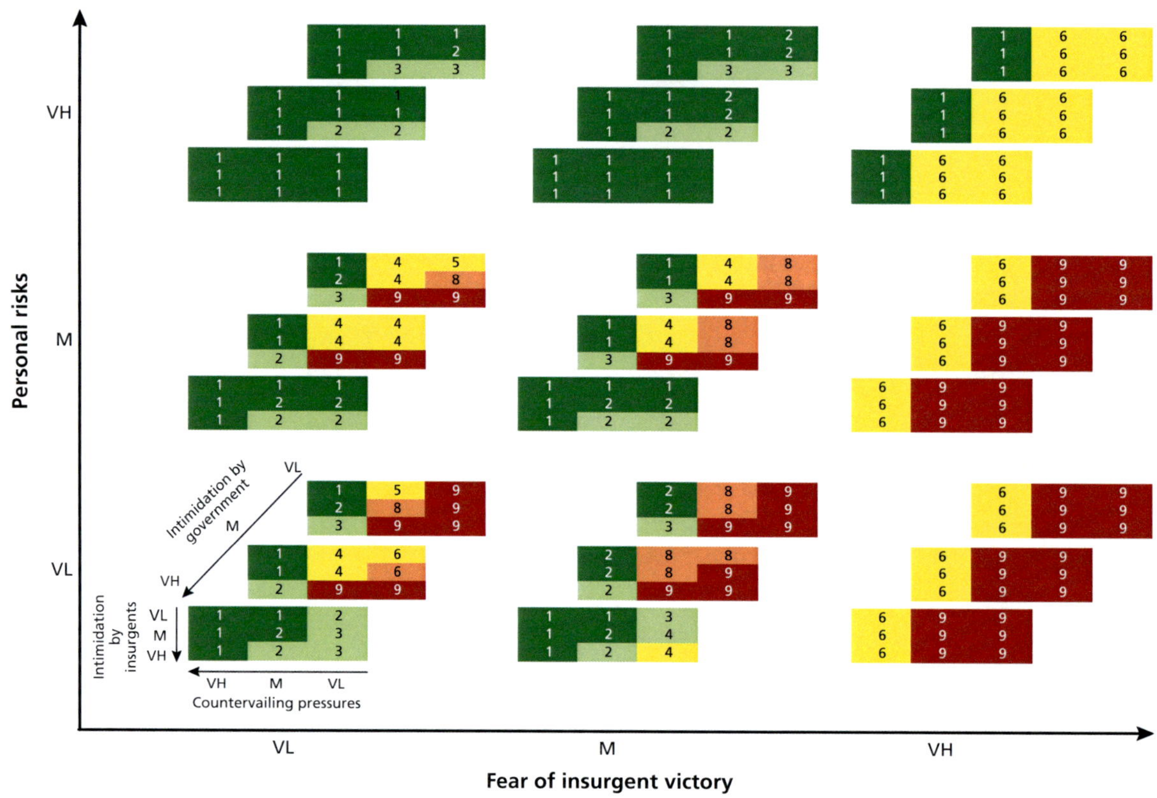

RAND *TR1220-4.4*

The astute reader will notice some striking differences between results for the two models. For example, in the top right corner, Acceptability of Risks is much lower for the Primary Factors model. The reason, simply, is that in that model, the result is driven by the public's principal fear.

CHAPTER FIVE

Using the Model for Knowledge Elicitation, Discussion, and Diagnosis

Our primary purpose in this report is to motivate and document PSOT. Applications must wait for future projects. In this chapter, however, we summarize some hopes, expectations, and results from very limited experiments using PSOT with researchers and students.

Expectations from Past Work

Based on experience prior to our model building we knew the following:

1. Factor trees themselves have proven quite useful in group discussions: Participants can quickly spot omitted influences and raise important issues about interactions and subtleties. Discussions are more productive than those without such structure and common visual focus.
2. Participants in group discussions can quickly grasp how to ask for changes of view about which variables of uncertainty analysis are highlighted and about how interaction effects are likely.
3. Participants in group discussions can quickly reason through why a result is as shown.
4. It seems to be possible for terrorism analysts to reach agreement rather easily about how to distinguish levels of the various factors meaningfully (i.e., what constitutes Very Low, Low, Medium, High, and Very High). Indeed, doing so was essential in empirical work done in 2010 and 2011 by RAND colleagues Kim Cragin, Todd Helmus, and Brian Jackson.

Lessons from Limited Experimentation

Before publishing our report, we wanted to do at least a modest amount of experimentation to see whether it would tend to confirm the hopes we had for the model. Thus, we briefed the model a number of times and conducted a few experiments that consisted of using the model to talk through specific cases of current or recent interest.* We learned that:

* We obtained feedback from RAND colleagues; the sponsoring offices; psychology-focused researchers in Defence Research and Development Canada (DRDC) (May 2012); the Computational Social-Sciences Working Group of the Military Operations Research Society (MORS); the HSCB FOCUS 2012 meeting sponsored by the DoD's Human Social, Cultural, and Behavioral Modeling program; doctoral students in the Pardee RAND Graduate School; and analysts working with the U.S. Marine Corps Combat Development Center.

- At least some subject-matter experts can relate easily to the model and sensibly estimate values of the input variables. By "sensibly," we mean that the character and meanings being ascribed to the values were as we intended.
- The model's computational results in experimental sessions had at least superficial face validity.
- The quality of discussion in experimental sessions was as intended, with more nuance and insight than is typical in less structured discussion.
- It was possible to communicate the concept of using the model first for diagnosis at a snapshot in time, and to then invert thinking about what factors must be affected to improve results and where the leverage lies for policy measures. Discussing what could reasonably be accomplished, or predicting degree of success in affecting the various levers of the problem, requires going beyond the model, but the model can identify or reaffirm qualitative notions about points of potential leverage.
- The quality of discussion was much enhanced by using the model for specific contexts, such as in Afghanistan, Iraq, or Yemen. Without context specificity, experts have more difficulty discussing the model and are less confident in their judgments (even generic judgments).

Perhaps the most important criticism (although it was less a criticism than a lament) was that the model was hard to assess without walking through one or several historical cases to see whether the model conveys a credible story. Working through historical cases would, in the future, be quite useful for validating the model.

With the conclusion about concreteness in mind (the last bulleted item) we see it as important for analysts/modelers to focus group discussion on concrete issues and contexts and to plan on doing more general analytical work themselves, including extrapolations and interpolations. That is, experts are better for brainstorming and spot-checking than for pulling things together.

We also learned a good deal about procedural challenges in using the model effectively. A major issue is how to allocate time between presenting background and basic concepts of the model, and actually discussing issues and soliciting knowledge or insights. Too much of the former amounts to a briefing rather than an exercise in eliciting information. Too little of the former results in the experts misinterpreting questions and, in particular, providing information that is very hard to interpret because of ambiguities caused by not having established the structure and semantics adequately. Our conclusion was that, because so many relevant experts have little if any background in causal modeling but significant familiarity with the very different mindsets of statistical methods and survey instruments, it is essential to have time for background and examples, so as to communicate the spirit of the exercise and the meaning of the information being sought. As a result, we concluded that work sessions should spend up to an hour for background and model discussion before actual work begins, perhaps after a break.

Conclusions

Although the effort was more time-consuming than we hoped, we were successful in building a prototype model using only a small number of building-block mathematical methods and in setting the model up for a combination of substantive discussion and debate and exploratory analysis.

Recommendations for Next Steps

Taken together, the prototype effort demonstrates the feasibility of markedly improving representation of social-science knowledge, eliciting knowledge from subject-matter experts, dealing with uncertainty, and working on the components of more composable models. Next steps could include the following:

1. Extensive experimentation applying the prototype model for reviews, substantive discussion, knowledge elicitation, and exploratory analysis for particular applications such as Afghanistan or elsewhere. This could be especially important now (2012) as part of pulling together knowledge before data disappear and memories fade.
2. Building additional "specification models" for other aspects of terrorism, insurgency, and irregular warfare. Each could be used on its own or become a module in more comprehensive system models.
3. Establishing efficient processes for exposing such models to peer review by the scholarly and operational communities, after which revised versions could be considered as vetted "modules" for model composition.

As a final observation, we note that an enormous amount of research has gone into the study of insurgency, terrorism, counterinsurgency, and counterterrorism over the past decade. However, the benefits of that and continuing research will depend strongly on integrative efforts—i.e., both conceptual and computational modeling. As we have emphasized throughout this report, we believe that such efforts must highlight uncertainties and disagreements, but at the same time assist the reaching of judgments and decisions. We see PSOT as a prototype for this kind of synthetic work.

APPENDIX A

Primer on Factor Trees (a reprint)

The following material (Davis, 2011) is reprinted by permission from the Society for Computer Simulation International. It was originally published in the Proceedings of the 2011 Winter Simulation Conference, edited by S. Jain, R.R. Creasey, J. Himmelspach, K.P. White, and M. Fu.

Abstract

Factor trees are relatively simple causal diagrams that indicate the many factors contributing to a phenomenon or effect at a snapshot in time. They consist of nodes and directional arcs (arrows) arranged in nearly hierarchical layers so that the effect can be seen as depending on a few high-level factors, but with those depending in turn on more detailed factors. This paper is a primer on building general and context-specialized factor trees; it includes subtleties and admonitions based on experience in several recent integrative studies on social science knowledge relating to terrorism, public support of insurgency and terrorism, and stabilization and reconstruction. It also discusses experiences with efforts to validate such conceptual models. Finally, the paper notes limitations and suggests supplementary methods.

1. Introduction

1.1. Background and Motivation

As RAND conducted a critical review of the scholarly social-science literature bearing on terrorism in 2008, it soon became evident that while the literature is quite rich, it is also fragmented and heterogeneous. The resulting book (Davis and Cragin, 2009) bore the subtitle "Putting the Pieces Together." In attempting the integration, we began with baby steps to maximize communication across professional boundaries and to limit goals to characterizing what is actually known or reasonably inferred, rather than merely speculated (Davis, 2009). We sought to identify the primary *factors* contributing to terrorism because specialists are very good at identifying factors—especially when their knowledge is pooled. We then arrayed those factors graphically in approximate "factor trees" so that readers or viewers could–at a glance—see the many factors at work and how they relate to each other. This was conceptual modeling, and a contribution toward generalized theory, but deliberately simplified.

Even initial factor trees can be good straw men to elicit further expression of knowledge and to stimulate discussion. Expert viewers will quickly and vociferously point out omissions and ambiguities—precisely what is sought in collaboration and review. The iterated factor trees can be very useful as *thinking models*—i.e., conceptual models to structure reasoning and, as appropriate, to inform building more complete models, including computer models (e.g., by informing the identification of objects, attributes, and processes to be included).

The early factor trees were well received by scholarly and applied audiences, officials, and senior military officers. However, analysts attempting to build new factor trees encountered difficulties. Some asked for a simple, down-to-earth primer. The result, this paper sponsored by the Human, Social, Cultural and Behavioral Modeling Program (HSCB), evolved over the course of two years with the benefit of a study for the Office of the Secretary of Defense on social science informing stabilization and reconstruction (Davis, 2011) and a study for the Joint Improvised Explosive Device Office (JIEDDO) on public support for insurgency and terrorism (Davis et al., forthcoming). RAND colleagues Kim Cragin, Todd Helmus, and Brian Jackson also completed studies on empirical work testing the factor trees of the earlier work on terrorism (Davis and Cragin, 2009). Robert Sheldon and colleagues, working for the U.S. Marine Corps Combat Development Command, has used an interesting variant of factor trees in their work, which they call influence factor diagrams (IFDs), in part to elicit expert information for specific contexts.

1.2. Structure of the Paper

Section 2 describes the basic concepts of factor trees briefly, in part reviewing prior discussions for the sake of being self-contained. Section 3 goes on to discuss more subtle aspects, including conventions and points of common difficulty. Section 4 illustrates factor trees motivated by the recent studies. These demonstrate how factor trees can convey different *kinds* of knowledge and how they can be specialized for particular contexts and compared across contexts. Section 5 discusses validation efforts. Section 6 gives brief conclusions.

2. The Basic Concepts

2.1. The Simplest Cases

In the simplest version (Figure 1a), a factor tree is laid out vertically with nodes connected by directional arcs (arrows) that point primarily upward. The top-most node D represents an effect (e.g., the propensity of someone to take an action). Lower-level nodes A, B, and C point to the top-most node, which means that they are factors contributing to that effect. They may themselves be effects of still lower-level factors as shown later.

As in Figure 1b, an arrow may bear a sign of +, -, or +/–; the absence of a sign means that a + sign applies. A positive arrow connecting two factors, say A and D, means that more of A will tend to mean more of D, and certainly not less. A negative sign means that the effect will tend to be reduced by more of the cause, but will certainly not be increased. A +/– sign implies that even the directionality of the effect is uncertain. In many instances, it is possible to avoid such an ambiguous influence by adding details—

i.e., replacing an ambiguous influence with two or more factors with individually unambiguous influences.

Figure 1: Simple Factor Trees

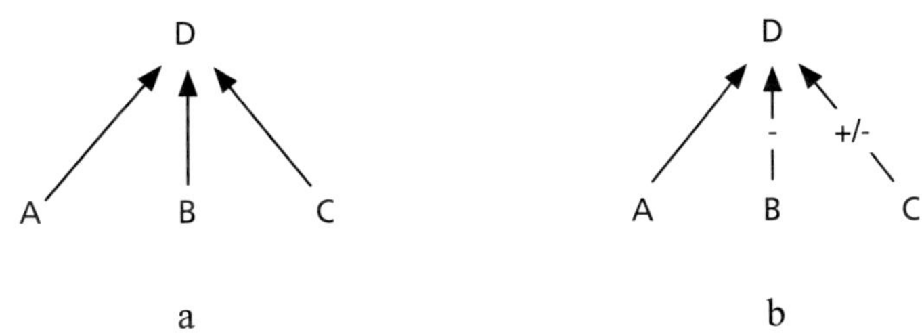

Unfortunately, it is not always possible to avoid the +/– ambiguities, especially in social science. One reason may be that we simply lack the information. For example, a particular leader may support or resist some activity when the time comes, but we don't yet know the leader's stance. A second reason may be that the phenomenon is afflicted by hidden variables with the result of apparent randomness.

The above discussion used the word "tend" because actual effects are context dependent. In Figure 1a, the effect of increasing A will depend on the values of B, C, and D (e.g., as in Figure 2). I have in mind that functional relationships will be semi-monotonic (non decreasing or non increasing). Although some articles in the social-science literature report inverted U-shapes, where an effect D first increases with A and then decreases, such findings are typically artifacts of hidden variables and relate to correlations rather than causality. For example, looking across many cases, countries with modest democratization may have more terrorism incidents than ones with none or Very High levels. A reason is likely to be that many of the countries with limited democratization also have weak security apparatuses (a hidden variable of the analysis).

Figure 2: A Factor's Influence Depends on the Other Factors' Values

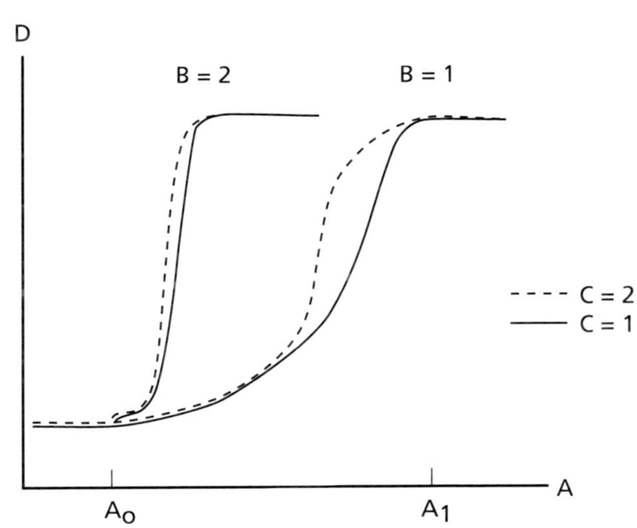

2.2. Approximate Combining Logic

We can sometimes add information on combining logic to the trees. To illustrate, suppose first that the nodes can have only binary values such as Yes, No. We can then add dashed, curved connector curves with "ands" or "ors" to indicate how factors tend to combine. Figure 3 shows several examples. If the factors are all binary, then in the leftmost figure, A, B, and C must all be present for the effect D to occur. In the middle figure, all that we know is that A, B, C, or some combination must be present. In the rightmost figure, C and either A or B must be present. If A, B, and C are all critical components, then they should be connected by "ands:" the absence of any one of them would mean that the effect will not happen. If they are substitutable for each other, then "ors" are appropriate. In political science such relationships are referred to in terms of "contingent" possibilities (George and Bennett, 2005). Considerable social-science analysis can be done with binary logic or fuzzy-logic extensions (Ragin, 2000; Ragin, 1989).

An important generalization interprets the "ands" and "ors" by whether the values of the various factors are or are not above thresholds of significance. Thus, A, B, and C need not be binary. For the leftmost case of "ands" in Figure 3 there would be no significant effect unless *all* factors exceed threshold values. Thresholds are common in social phenomena (e.g., critical-mass effects). Analytically, use of thresholds sometimes allows us to treat effects of nonlinear phenomena with an initial filter (a *product* of factors) and subsequent linear-weighted sums. This can be used in social-science modeling (Davis, 2006).

Figure 3: Factor Trees with First-Order Combining Logic

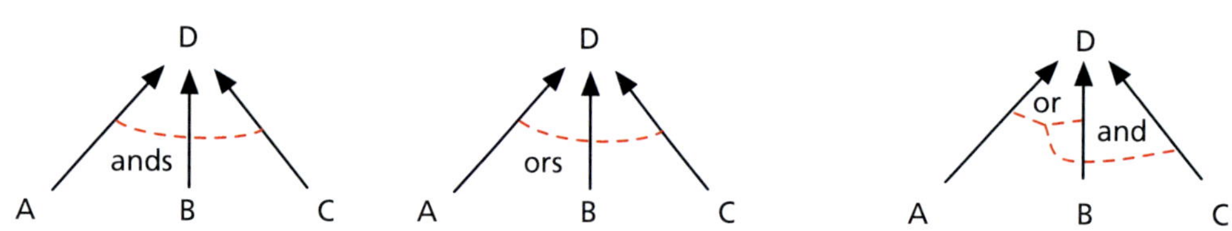

2.3. Feedback and Other Aspects of Dynamics

As most readers will appreciate, describing many systems of interest requires worrying about dynamics. Corresponding diagrammatic depictions can become complicated quickly, however. The elegant influence diagrams of System Dynamics (Forrester, 1961; Sterman, 2000), for example, may seem like a mere blur (or even a "fur ball") to those unfamiliar with them. For the sake of good two-way communication with heterogeneous audiences, including many social scientists with no background in system work, our factor trees normally suppress dynamics (by exception, feedbacks can be shown with backward pointing dashed arrows). The point is not to deny dynamic effects, but rather to focus attention on the causal influences in effect "now." Factor trees show factors at work at a snapshot in time. Technically, this is often reasonable because many aspects of a system's dynamics have effects over relatively long time scales and, thus, can be separable. A second reason is that the opposite case may apply: feedbacks may occur so quickly as to be not worth troubling about. If a system equilibrates quickly, we need not agonize about the processes by which it does so. This said, the argument is to deal with dynamics separately when possible, not to ignore them. But for the distracting effects of doing so, it would be good practice to annotate factor-tree charts with a footnote such as:

This diagram reflects causal influences at a snapshot in time. Significantly later values of factors may depend on earlier values of many other factors on the tree. That is, interactions over time may be many, significant, and highly cross-cutting.

2.4. Imperfect Hierarchies and Unequal Influences

The term "factor tree" arose because we aspired to diagrams that were approximately hierarchical: such diagrams are very useful for both analysis and discussion. The idea, in many strands of work, is that we need a high-level view of the whole (breadth), but to "understand" and stay out of trouble we also need the ability to drill down into detail ("zoom"). This is arguably a design principle for high-level decision support (Davis, Shaver, and Beck, 2008). It is especially feasible with hierarchical decomposition, whether in social science or, say, systems engineering.

Significantly, factor trees need not be purely hierarchical and seldom can be in a rigorous description: the real world being modeled is just too complicated. In Figure 4a, E influences both B and C, thereby making the "tree" a bit bushy. In addition, there may be some factors I and J that influence many or all of the higher-level factors. These are like "global variables" in programming, and are shown at the bottom of the factor tree in one or more boxes.

Often, the factors influencing an effect are not equally important and it may be possible to make useful qualitative distinctions. Figure 4b illustrates this for two different cases (i.e., different contexts, as when one is discussing issues in one country or another), one in which A and B are much stronger influences on D than is C; and one in which C is the much stronger influence. In both cases, D depends ultimately on A,G,E, and H; but E's effect on D is small except through its influence on B. If the linkage of E to C is ignored, then the diagram is strictly hierarchical except for the global variables I and J. As in multiresolution modeling generally, approximations are liberating (Davis, 2003).

If the cross-branch interactions are too numerous, or the global factors too dominating, the concept of the factor tree becomes dubious. Some systems are best depicted differently (e.g., social-networks systems or hub-and-spoke systems). Fortunately, many complex systems in the real world are "nearly decomposable" with important hierarchical features (Simon, 1981). Even highly networked systems often have hierarchical features.

Figure 4: Approximately Hierarchical Trees for Different Cases

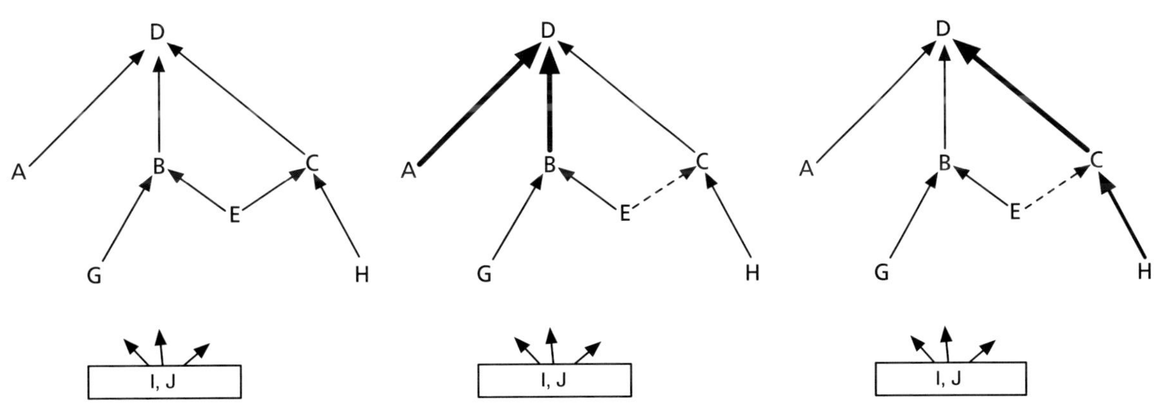

a

b (for two different cases or contexts)

3. What Causes Difficulty? Subtleties and Admonitions

In the course of the last 2–3 years, my colleagues and I have had numerous opportunities to use factor-tree methods, and to engage with analysts in other organizations who have also adopted the methods. Not surprisingly, a number of puzzles and complications arose, and some things that seemed intuitively obvious at first proved less obvious to others. What follows are suggestions based on that experience.

3.1. Distinguishing between General and Specific Factor Trees

The factor trees that I had in mind in our original work (Davis and Cragin, 2009) were intended to be relatively general—a kind of "general theory lite." A major purpose was to incorporate factors and causal pathways that were usually discussed separately and narrowly. Any such general depiction, however, will necessarily be abstract. This is very satisfying to some, but not to those who would prefer to see only those factors applying in a specific context of interest and with those factors expressed as concretely as possible (e.g., referring to a particular strength of a particular tribe in a particular region and time).

What has been confusing, sometimes, is how the general and specific relate to each other. A factor tree intended to be general will include factors that do not apply in some of the specific contexts of interest. A general factor tree, then, may be good as a *starting point* for a context-specific application (a kind of template). When used as a starting point, the intention is that the factor tree indicate what factors to look for, i.e., what kinds of factors *might* be important in the particular context. In an application, it might quickly be concluded that only a subset are in fact significant, at which point the factor tree could be simplified in scope but made more concrete in other respects. The general factor tree, however, can also be seen as suggesting what additional factors could in the future *become* important for the particular context. That is, it may help anticipate changes, to recognize them when they occur, to head off possibilities before they become troublesome, and to recognize and exploit positive opportunities. It is for such reasons that general theory is powerful and fundamentally different in kind from what is often called "theory," but is actually something far more narrow (what might be called a "theory-oid" by analogy with "factoid."

My caution here, then, is that even those who are focused on a particular context and need a high degree of specificity to operate can benefit greatly from working back and forth between relatively more general and relatively more specific conceptual models.

3.2. What Factor Trees Are Not

One of the most common errors in trying to use factor trees is to confuse them with other graphical methods. Factor trees are not stock-flow diagrams in the sense of System Dynamics, although they are related to what System Dynamics calls causal loops (Sterman, 2000) and most factors are akin to "stocks" in system dynamics. As suggested by its name, System Dynamics emphasizes dynamics (especially feedbacks) and broad system views. Factor trees suppress dynamics and may pertain to only one "module" of phenomena.

Factor trees are also not the influence diagrams of *Bayesian-net or influence-net models*, where the nodes are characterized by probabilities or probability distributions

(Rosen and Smith, 1996; Wagenhals, Levis, and Halder, 2006). Ordinarily, the factors are characterized only by quantity or degree. This said, there is an intellectual relationship between the two methods and much of the thinking that goes on in factor-tree work could be carried over into Bayesian-net or influence-net modeling. Indeed, both the current work with factor trees and early influence-net modeling drew upon my own multiresolution qualitative modeling of decisionmaking in the early 1990s (Davis and Arquilla, 1991) as cited in the Rosen-Smith article.

Factor trees are most decidedly not *decision-analysis* trees. The nodes are not decision points with branches corresponding to different decision outcomes. Those who are familiar and comfortable with decision trees may find themselves trying to twist factor trees into that kind of representation. Doing so is a mistake although, as shown later, the factors affecting a decision can readily be shown and the top-most node (the "effect") can be something like the likelihood of a particular decision.

Factor trees are not strategies-to-task (STT) decompositions of the sort used in defense work (Kent and Simons, 1991), but they may have a significant intellectual relationship. An STT diagram has an objective or strategy at the top. It then identifies all of the component actions to be taken (or the corresponding subordinate objectives), and the components of those, recursively, until—at the lowest level—it identifies concrete "tasks" to be accomplished, such as closing an airfield or mining a maritime choke point. This said, many STT constructs can be mapped into corresponding factor trees by reconceptualizing objectives and subordinate objectives as variables with quantity or degree. For example, if the military mission to be accomplished is expressed as a verb, such as "Halt an invading army," and if the STT construct identities different organizational submissions and tasks, the problem can be reconceptualized as a factor tree with "Depth of the invader's penetration before being stopped" as the top node, which would be determined by factors such as the defender's resources and capabilities, operational strategy, command and control, and execution effectiveness. A computational model for assessing related capabilities can described with what is essentially a factor tree, with many levels (Davis, McEver, and Wilson, 2002).

For social scientists, another type of confusion arises because social scientists are steeped in statistical methods where a "model" is typically a regression equation used to infer correlations among variables observed in data. That is often very different from representing causality, although the gap can be narrowed using econometric methods if the data is rich and the experiments controlled (Angrist and Pischke, 2009). Nonetheless, even econometricians think about causality differently than I do in this paper because they tend to be data-driven rather than theory-driven. Causality is a deep issue in science, mathematics, and the philosophy of science (Pearl, 2009; Dowe, 2008). In some systems work, the concept of causality is weakened because of feedbacks: ultimately, everything is related to everything. In that case, we may wish to see causality as something more local in time than fundamental.

3.3. Admonitions for Those Building Factor Trees

People using factor trees will find their own way, but the following items constitute some advice.

3.3.1. The Importance of Words

Factor trees are fundamentally mechanisms for communication. Their success or failure depends on the words used to identify the factors. It is crucial in factor-tree work to name the nodes carefully and with a premium on intuitive concepts. Some of the attributes of such naming include:

- Brevity
- Pointedness (e.g., "revenge" rather than "ill feelings," if revenge is really the point)
- Nouns rather than, say, the verbs that might be used in a decomposition identifying actions
- Plain-language terminology in preference to specialized jargon or academese

Unfortunately, many words that we think to use have multiple meanings, sometimes in conflict with each other (antagonyms), some with insidious baggage. A factor such as "room for compromise" might suggest something good, or—to other people—the potential for the abandonment of principles. Using "fundamentalist beliefs" as a factor can usefully highlight the role of black-and-white thinking and related intolerance, but such a name could be offensive to some. A compromise in that case might be "Fundamentalism and active intolerance." It would convey the point that most of those holding fundamentalist beliefs do not actively seek to deny others their own beliefs, or to interfere with their lives.

3.3.2. Distinguishing Factor Trees from Decompositions

A source of much difficulty in building factor trees has been the tendency to confuse factors with components. The syntax to remember is that of a function. In Figure 1, D is a function of the factors (independent variables) A, B, and C. It might also be the case that D can be broken down into components. These might represent, for example, geography, gender, age, or ethnicity. The problem here is that, if one starts showing "components," diagrams can quickly become cluttered and more confusing than helpful.

Some guidance here is

- When discussing factors, think of them in terms of "contribute to" or "are independent variables determining," rather than "is a part of."
- Do not distinguish between components unless the distinction needs to be highlighted.
- Do not distinguish between components that change by the same processes (albeit with different parameter values).
- Think of the factors as multi-dimensional arrays.

This last item may remind readers of the virtues of specialized modeling systems such as Analytica (Lumina Corporation), which encourage thinking and modeling in terms of arrays, rather than scalars. Just as the beauty of Newton's Laws, Maxwell's equations, or Einstein's general relativity theory are evident only when such notation in used, so also the fundamental character of many policy-analytic and social-science phenomena are best understood by using such arrays (Morgan and Henrion, 1992). A military example is illustrated in Davis, McEver, and Wilson, 2002. Unfortunately, this chunking does not come easily in most programming languages, even if it is permitted.

3.3.3. Comprehensiveness of Factor Sets (Factors versus Bulleted Items)

Although there are no laws governing use of factor trees, it is good practice to assure that the factors affecting a given node are as "complete a set" as possible. If one can think of some factors, but it is clear that they are merely what is coming to mind at the moment, then it is better to list them as bulleted items rather than as nodes. This has the practical benefit of allowing a factor tree to show some familiar items without undercutting the intellectual integrity of the whole. The bulleted items are examples, and can be tailored to particular audiences if need be, but the node structure should have rigor and staying power.

How do we know what is "comprehensive?" One way is to cheat, by adding a factor "other." That is actually preferable to conveying the misimpression that a set of factors is complete when one knows it is not. More seriously however, there is no formula for assessing completeness in subjects such as social science. Consider, however, the old wisdom that concluding guilt of murder requires demonstrating motive, opportunity, and means. Are there other things that ought to be required? Perhaps, but this set has proven itself over centuries (perhaps millennia) as a good approximation of a complete set of criteria. Section 4 gives examples of factor trees and readers can muse about whether the factors at a level appear to be rather complete.

3.3.4. Reading Left to Right and Dealing with Overlaps

Some natural factors have potentially overlapping scope. A mechanism for dealing with this potential problem economically is constructing and reading the factor trees left to right so that a factor's scope is regarded as picking up only considerations not covered by the preceding factors (those to the left). As an example, two factors might be "enthusiasm for group" and "inspiration by group's leader." If these were shown side by side, the latter would be interpreted as the incremental additional inspiration associated with the leader rather than the group (the reverse ordering might be more appropriate in some cases). This approach conveys a sense of causality or precondition from left to right, which can be useful as part of a narrative that accompanies a factor tree. In a sense, it also builds in some dynamics unobtrusively.

4. Examples for Diverse Applications

The purpose of this section is to illustrate how factor trees have been used for what are really very different purposes, although with overlaps. The examples are based on finished studies.

4.1. Alternative Causal Pathways to Terrorism

The factor-tree methodology was developed for a study reviewing the social science relevant to understanding terrorism and counterterrorism (Davis and Cragin, 2009). The study included a comprehensive literature survey, but then had the challenge of integrating results in an understandable way, despite major differences across the scholarly community and even more differences within the communities involved with strategy, policy, and counterterrorism operations. A particularly insidious problem was the tendency of many toward single-factor explanations, as when it was asserted—for a time—that "the problem" was the madrasas that teach violent jihad, that "the problem" was Islam, or that "the problem was irrationality." Serious scholars of terrorism knew better and counseled against such would-be explanations, but their answering questions with "Well, it depends," were sometimes not appreciated. Our study sought to be both synthetic and analytic. An important virtue of factor trees is that they can juxtapose alternative causal pathways—i.e., what political scientists call equifinality (George and Bennett, 2005).

4.1.1. Root Causes Of Terrorism

The first factor tree appearing in our study addressed root causes of terrorism, a subject fraught with controversy. Figure 5 from a chapter by Darcy Noricks was our way of pulling together the many different streams. The factor tree has three levels of detail, with some cross-cutting factors and even some global factors. It also has some "and" conditions and some "or" conditions. The top level of the tree implies that, to a first approximation, the root-cause likelihood of terrorism depends on the culture countenancing violence, having grievances, and having mechanisms to organize and support those who might be willing to use terrorism. At lower levels, the combining rules are all shown as of the "or" variety. The reason for countenancing violence might be cultural, ideological, political (as in response to repression of an illegitimate regime), foreign occupation, or some combination. All of the higher-level factors could be affected by a low capacity for governance, among other things (one of the global variables below). Globalization is shown as a cross-cutting factor affecting economics, modernization, and social instability.

Figure 5: Root Causes of Terrorism

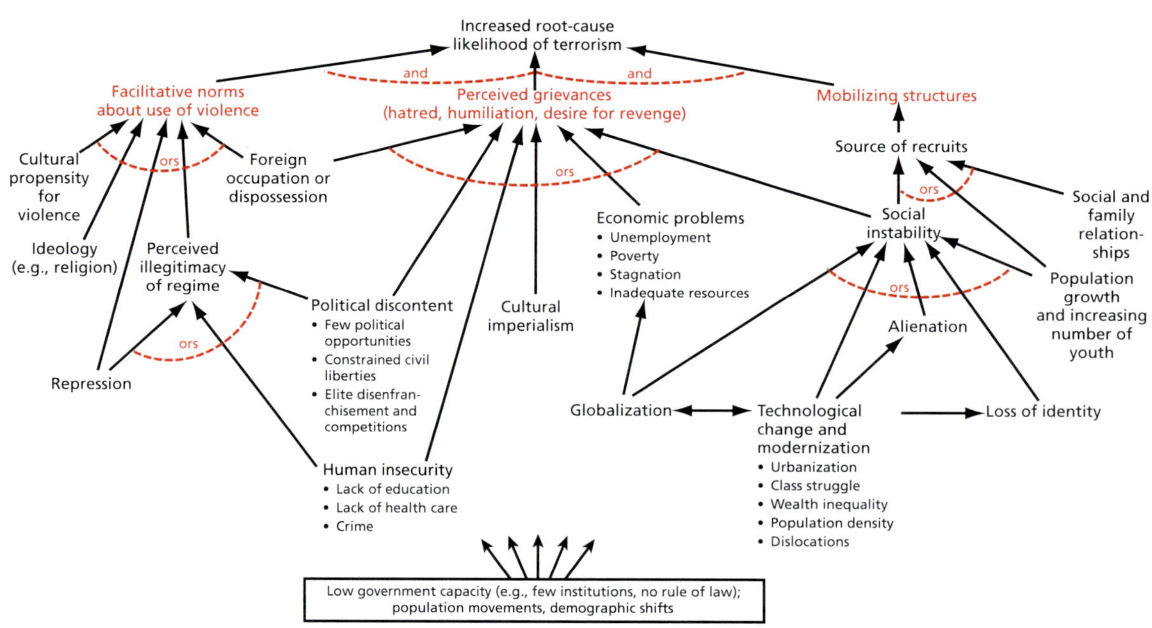

RAND *TR1220-A.5*

The point here is that instead of taking sides in the debate about whether "the problem" is the culture, economics, globalization, or whatever, the enlightened view is that the propensity for terrorism can depend on any or all of them. To be sure, in a particular place at a particular time, some influences may be stronger than others, but no one explanation doesn't apply generally The narrative that accompanied this factor tree included the observation that grievances exist in all societies. Terrorism, however, is seldom the result. There has to be a willingness to use terrorist violence and, as a practical matter, there needs to be a mechanism, such as an organization with the competence to plan and execute operations. This is not always true (yes, there are lone wolves), but it is usually true: most people who might have the grievances and willingness lack the opportunity, knowledge, or competence.

Referring back to Section 3, we might ask whether the factors at the second level are "comprehensive." They are intended to be, at least when supplemented by global variables such as those in the bottom box. They are probably not as comprehensive as intended, but they are certainly not ad hoc.

One of the rules mentioned above is, however, violated in the tree: the phrase "facilitative norms about use of violence" is unquestionably an example of academese. Compromises occur in collaborative writing and did in the case of this factor tree.

4.1.2. Motivations in Terrorism

A second use of factor trees in the same volume was a summary depiction of what causes individuals or groups to participate in terrorism. Figure 6, from a chapter by Todd Helmus, shows the factor tree for individual willingness to engage in terrorism. Some of the factors relate strongly to perceptions, needs, and even passions. They may, however, be affected by global factors such as a charismatic terrorist leader (Osama bin Laden was the obvious example early in this decade, inspiring many youths to join the violent jihad). As another observation, some terrorists are motivated by religious or otherwise ideological considerations, but others are motivated by very different matters, such as the excitement of joining other young men in taking risky "heroic" actions. These different motivations, then, are different causal pathways. One of the topics discussed with this factor tree was an ongoing academic debate between terrorist experts who argued that many terrorists arise from actions of a "bunch of guys getting together" (Sageman, 2008) and others arguing that there was much more top-down recruiting than the others recognized (Hoffman, 2008). In fact, both mechanisms can be observed and it is not good science to pick "the most popular explanation." There are temptations to do so in social science, however, because simple explanations ("ultimately, it's about such-and-such") often gain attention.

Figure 6: Individual Motivations for Terrorism

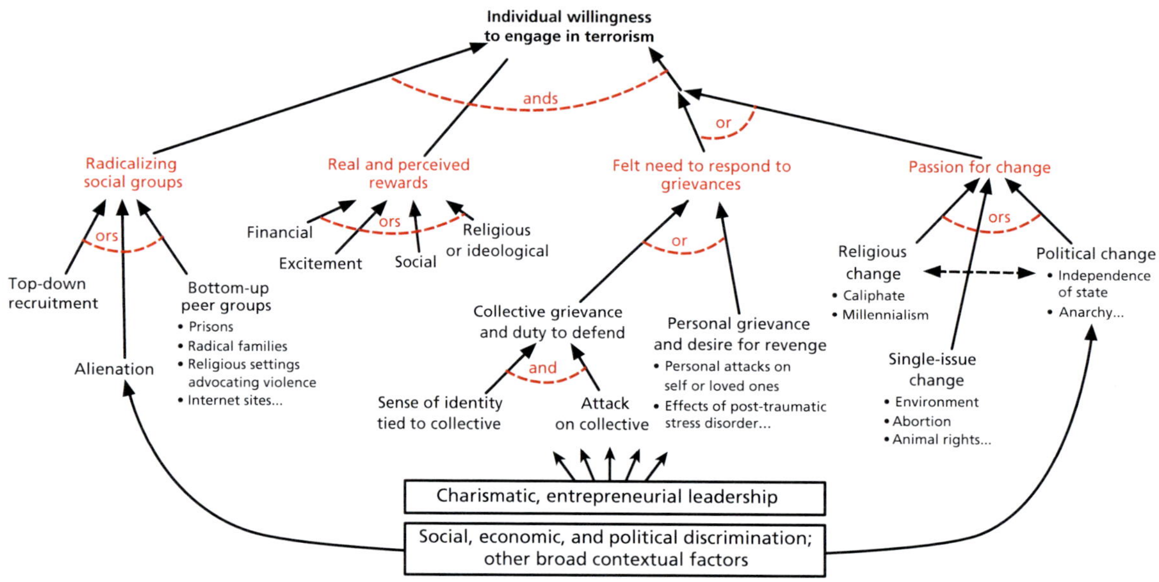

SOURCE: Adapted from Helmus (2009).
RAND *TR1220-A.6*

4.2. Factors in Decisions

Although factor trees are not decision trees, they can be used to illuminate what goes into decisions.

4.2.1. Behavior of Terrorist Organizations

Figure 7, from a chapter of the same study by Brian Jackson, shows the factors believed to influence the decision making of a terrorist organization. Jackson was drawing from a multidisciplinary literature on decision making as well as such information as could then be obtained about terrorist decision making itself. Although the model was based largely on rational-actor theory, it also allows for "irrationalities" due to, e.g., misperceptions, dissension, and lack of information. Some of the items highlighted by Jackson are often not mentioned in discussions of how terrorist organizations make decisions, although they are well grounded. One is that such organizations worry about resources, not just money, but also, e.g., their supply of people with specialized skills (bomb-making?) and know-how. They also worry about the consequences on the proposed action on group cohesiveness: will the proposed act inspire the organization or cause it to splinter? In reality, major debates go on within terrorist organizations.

Figure 7: Factors in Terrorist-Organization Decision Making

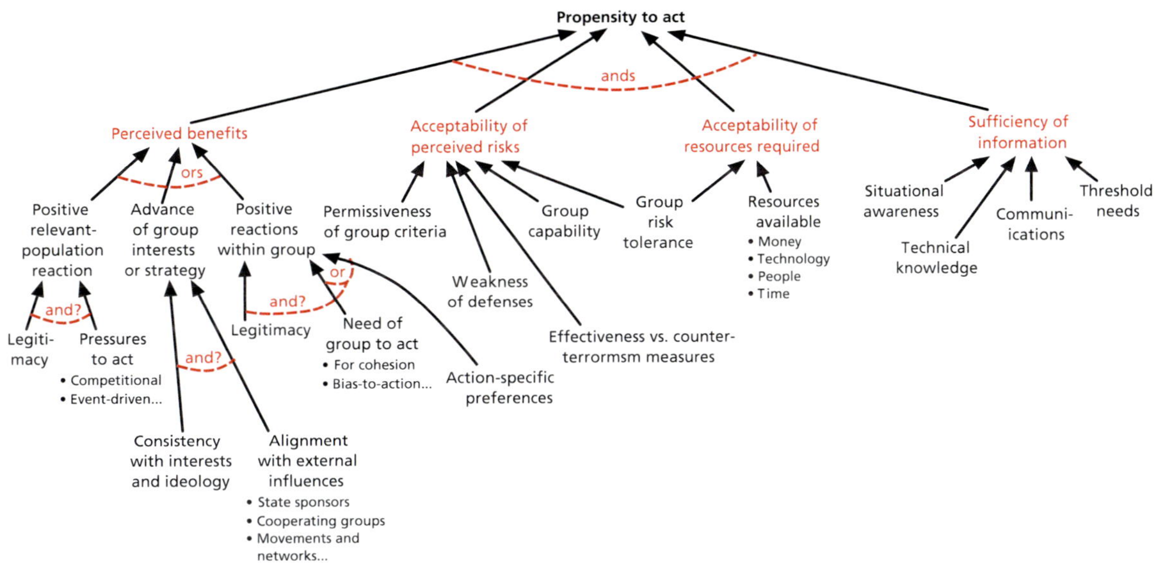

RAND *TR1220-A.7*

4.2.2. Insurgent Decisionmaking on Peace and War Decisions

Figure 8 comes a chapter by Christopher Chivvis and me in a more recent study on the social science of stabilization and reconstruction (Davis, 2011). It reduced a great deal of discussion in the literature to a matter of a relatively easy-to-understand decision. In a post-conflict situation in which intervenors are hoping that insurgents will negotiate, the insurgents may be driven by a superficially rational-analytic decision: is it "smart" to negotiate or go back to war? As the figure indicates, the matter is actually not simple. Real people are not economists who believe that the rational decision is that which maximizes the expected future utility. Instead, they worry not just about the expected outcome (i.e., the mean of a distribution if the outcome could be described probabilistically), but about the upside opportunities and downside risks (Davis, Kulick, and Egner, 2005). Negotiation might mean peace and prosperity, or it might mean that the last hope of their cause would be dashed as the dominant power reneges on promises. Going back to war might possibly lead to glorious victory, but it might instead mean utter annihilation. Further, real people are affected by greed, exhaustion, and other beyond-rational considerations. Experienced negotiators understand these matters, even if they do not usually express them in analytic ways.

In viewing this tree, the reader should note our attempt to have factors at a level be comprehensive. We have factors not just for best estimate judgments, but for perceived upside opportunities and downside risks. We also include explicitly a set of factors relating to beyond-rational considerations. Is this complete? Perhaps, perhaps not, but it is surely much more so than the usual model dealing only with so-called rational-analytic reasoning based on maximizing expected utility. Note also that bulleted items are mere examples, and almost obviously not complete sets.

Figure 8: Decision on Whether To Go Back To War

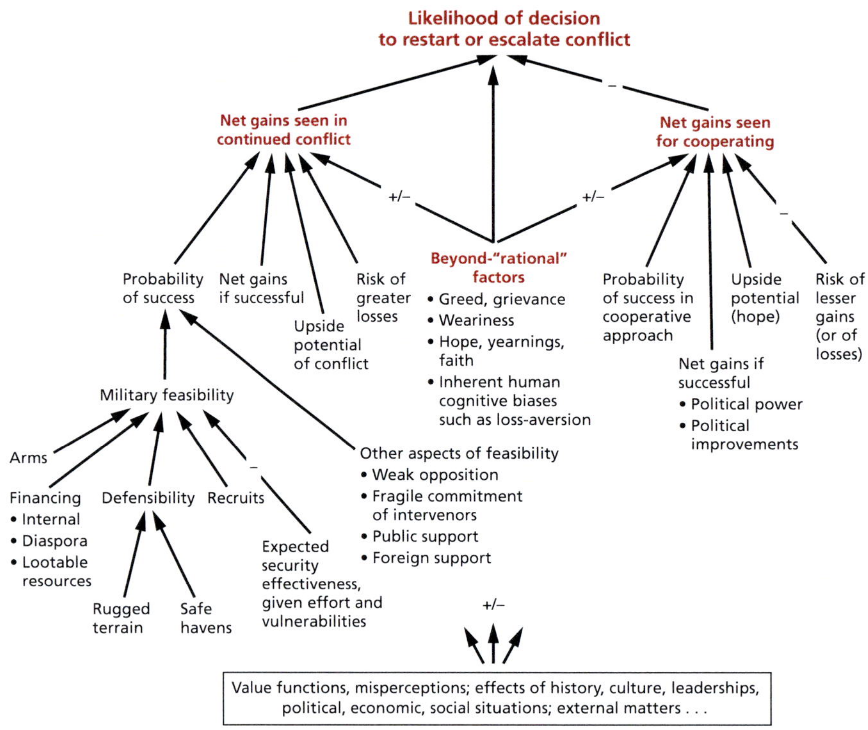

NOTE: The factors apply at a snapshot in time.
RAND *TR1220-A.8*

4.3. Factor Trees To Show Crucial Distinctions and Components

Although I usually advise against using factor trees to discuss components, there are exceptions. Two examples are worth mentioning briefly. Figure 9 shows a factor tree from a chapter by Elizabeth Wilke, me, and Christopher Chivvis on achieving trust and cooperation in a post-conflict environment that includes a great deal of anger and bitterness. Here the narrative that goes with the picture is that it is crucial to distinguish between the kind of trust that comes from pragmatic calculations and the kind of trust that comes from personal relationships. The former may be shallow and even cynical, but may be quite feasible to achieve and effective. For example, a given faction may trust another faction because it sees that it is the other faction's interest to cooperate, especially if third-party intervenors are present to help assure that assessment of interests. There is nothing naïve about that. In contrast, the aspiration of building deeper relations-based trust is one to be realized over years or even decades, and may simply not come about. The chapter's story, then, is that attending to social issues is a crucial element of stabilization and reconstruction, that progress is achievable, but that the shorter-term payoffs will likely come from finding and exploiting opportunities where interest will overlap. This is not just sensible, but well grounded in empirical social science. The factor tree dramatizes the distinction between types of trust.

Figure 9: Factor Trees Merely Highlighting Distinctions or Components

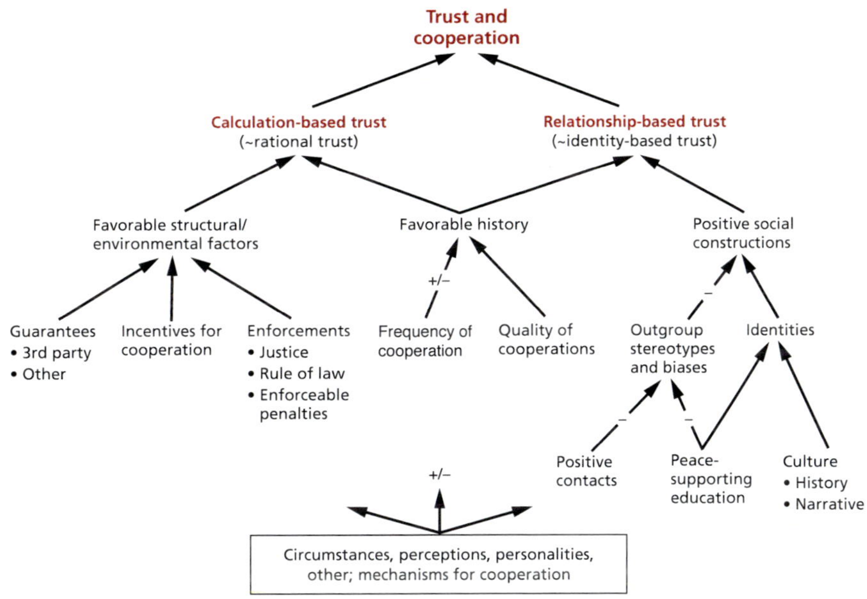

NOTE: The factors apply at a snapshot in time.
RAND *TR1220-A.9*

5. Validation and Limitations

5.1. Validation

If factor trees are to be seen as conceptual models, how can they be evaluated, or even "validated?" Validation of social-science models is not like validating physics models, for many reasons that should be obvious. Nonetheless, much can be done. In our recent study on public support for insurgency and terrorism (Davis et al., forthcoming), and in work by colleagues, we concluded that much can be done with case studies relating to validation and simultaneous theory improvement. The approach taken in the case studies, however, is a combination of testing and theory development, along the lines urged by the late Alexander George, who pioneered systematic case-study approaches (George and Bennett, 2005). Key elements in our approach were as follows:

Tentative Confirmation of Factors. Empirical information can indicate whether the factors identified in the conceptual models appear to be at work in real-world cases as judged by, e.g., polls, accounts by reporters interviewing members of the public, the study of diaries and records, the voluminous writings of insurgent leaders, and so on. If the factors show up, this is useful incremental confirmation, although not proof. If the factors arise in a way conveying roughly the same narrative as the conceptual model, then the sense of confirmation is enhanced.

Tentative Confirmation Regarding Causality and Necessity. As discussed earlier, factor-tree models are causal models; they distinguish between sets of factors that are all necessary (at least in a first approximation) for an effect to occur and those that may be individually sufficient. Empirical information can provide tentative confirmation on both of these matters. The accumulation of such confirmations encourages confidence, especially if—once again—the empirical work also supports the causal explanations that are being given.

Falsification and Supplementation. If factors arising in such empirical information are not in the conceptual models, then the models are, in a sense, falsified—a key element of science. The "in a sense" phrase applies because there is no shame in having a model that does well in most respects but needs to be improved with additional factors—so long as, over time, the number of factors does not continue to grow without bound. The primary downside is that doing so entangles model-building and testing—something unavoidable at this stage of research. In one study my colleagues and I did a fair amount of supplementing, particularly as regards the mechanisms that factions use in attempting to influence public support. That is, although the empirical work confirmed the factors we had identified, it suggested that some of the causal paths were better depicted with different lower-level arrangement of factors. Most notably, we concluded that in understanding insurgency it is often more apt to highlight the factor of identity in the causal chain of motivation than to try to disentangle influences of religion, culture, nationalism, and tribalism.

Similarly, if the narratives reported from empirical sources describe cause-effect relationships differently than do the models, then this might be another type of falsification (if the empirical sources' narrative is credible), as would be evidence that a factor shown by the model as necessary is often not necessary. Such evidence can motivate refinements in the evolving model

5.2. Limitations of the Factor-Tree Approach

As mentioned at the outset, factor trees convey a snapshot view of causal factors at work. They do not describe dynamics (except in subtle ways). Further, they inevitably reflect the author's perspective or preferred representation. Some natural supplements to factor trees are qualitative influence diagram and case tables (Davis, 2011, Chapter 8). More ambitious, of course, would be building models that run, i.e., models that specify the algorithms by which factors combine and thus provide some predictive capability (Davis, 2006), although that should be understood only in the sense of better understanding the odds of different developments, with considerable attention paid to remaining humble.

6. Final Observations

Much has been learned about using factor trees over the last 2–3 years, and also how to think about validating them as conceptual models. My judgment, and that of colleagues, is that they have proven quite useful. As experienced modelers and analysts would expect, however, they prove to be one useful tool in a tool kit, especially for social science, but other tools are essential as well—and sometimes better.

References

Angrist, Joshua D., and Jorn-Steffen Pischke 2009. *Mostly Harmless Econometrics: An Empiricist's Companion*. Princeton, N.J.: Princeton University Press.

Davis, Paul K. 2003."Exploratory Analysis and Implications for Modeling," in *New Challenges, New Tools*, edited by Stuart Johnson, Martin Libicki, and Gregory Treverton, 255–283. Santa Monica, Calif.: RAND Corporation.

——— 2006. "A Qualitative Multiresolution Model for Counterterrorism." In *Proceedings of the SPIE*.

——— 2009. "Specifying the Content of Humble Social Science Models." In *Proceedings of the 2009 Summer Computer Simulation Conference*, Istanbul, Turkey.

——— 2011 (ed.), *Dilemmas of Intervention: Social Science for Stabilization and Reconstruction*, Santa Monica, Calif.: RAND Corporation.

Davis, Paul K., and John Arquilla 1991. *Deterring Or Coercing Opponents in Crisis: Lessons From the War With Saddam Hussein*, Santa Monica, Calif.: RAND Corporation.

Davis, Paul K., and Kim Cragin (eds.) 2009. *Social Science for Counterterrorism: Putting the Pieces Together*, Santa Monica, Calif.: RAND Corporation.

Davis, Paul K., Jonathan Kulick, and Michael Egner 2005. *Implications of Modern Decision Science for Military Decision Support Systems*. Santa Monica, Calif.: RAND Corporation.

Davis, Paul K. et al. forthcoming. *Understanding and Influencing Public Support for Insurgency and Terrorism*. Santa Monica, Calif.: RAND Corporation.

Davis, Paul K., Jimmie McEver, and Barry Wilson 2002. *Measuring Interdiction Capabilities in the Presence of Anti-access Strategies: Exploratory Analysis to Inform Adaptive Strategies for the Persian Gulf*, Santa Monica, Calif.: RAND Corporation, MR-1471-AF.

Davis, Paul K., Russell D. Shaver, and Justin Beck 2008. *Portfolio-Analysis Methods for Assessing Capability Options*. Santa Monica, Calif.: RAND Corporation.

Dowe, Phil 2008. "Causal Processes." In *The Stanford Encyclopedia of Philosophy (Fall 2008 Edition)*, edited by Edward N. Zalta.

Forrester, Jay W. 1961. *Industrial Dynamics*. Cambridge, Mass.: M.I.T. Press.

George, Alexander L., and Andrew Bennett 2005. *Case Studies and Theory Development in the Social Sciences*. Cambridge, Mass.: MIT Press.

Hoffman, Bruce 2008. "The Myth of Grass-Roots Terrorism," *Foreign Affairs*, May/June, 133–38.

Kent, Glenn A., and William E. Simons 1991. *A Framework for Enhancing Operational Capabilities*. Santa Monica, Calif.: RAND Corporation.

Morgan, M. Granger, and Max Henrion 1992. *Uncertainty: A Guide to Dealing With Uncertainty in Quantitative Risk and Policy Analysis*. New York: Cambridge University Press.

Pearl, Judea 2009. *Causality: Models, Reasoning, and Inference*, Cambridge, Mass.: Cambridge University Press.

Ragin, Charles C., 1989. *The Comparative Method: Moving Beyond Qualitative and Quantitative Strategies*. University of California Press.

——— 2000. *Fuzzy-Set Social Science*. Chicago: University of Chicago Press.

Rosen, Julie A., and Wayne L. Smith 1996. "Influence Net Modeling With Causal Strengths: An Evolutionary Approach." In *Proceedings of 1996 Command and Control Research and Technology Symposium*, https://www.inet.saic.com/docs/_docs_/math.pdf.

Simon, Herbert A. 1981. *Sciences of the Artificial, 2nd Edition*. Cambridge, Mass.: MIT Press.

Sterman, John D. 2000. *Business Dynamics: Systems Thinking and Modeling for a Complex World*. Boston: McGraw-Hill.

Wagenhals, Lee W., Alexander E. Levis, and Saijad Halder 2006. *Planning Execution, and Assessment of Effects-Based Operations (EBO).* Fairfax, Va.: George Mason University, AFRL-IF-RS-TR–2006-176.

APPENDIX B

Verification and Validation

This appendix discusses verification and validation briefly.

Verification

Verification is assuring that a model implements faithfully what is intended. Model quality is sometimes seriously affected by programming problems that appear only when the model is used away from its "baseline case."

Our use of a high-level language that exploits arrays and modularity to build a specification model has at least two major advantages in this regard.

Reading the code is greatly simplified because equations that might otherwise have to be copied in multiple places with corresponding maintenance problems often appear in a single place. Just as library functions improve verifiability, so also can array equations. Having them in the specification model will likely encourage anyone who chooses to reprogram to make use of array features in his preferred language, even if they are not customarily used in that language.

Establishing verification-related testing functions can be accomplished easily using the same array machinery, and accomplished by "mere mortals" rather than only by expert programmers. Doing so is analogous to what researchers do when they set up extra columns in a spreadsheet program so that they can test calculations step by step, even though those test-related columns are subsequently hidden.

Figure B.1 shows a diagnostics table laying out the step-by-step elements of PSOT's calculations of Acceptability of Costs and Risks, with each of the three alternative models used for that purpose. The inputs at the top can be varied systematically as one inspects the step-by-step results for errors, which often stand out (e.g., typos often create error messages). Other displays, of course, would be graphical, which can be quite helpful in doing top-down verification—looking for odd top-level results and then drilling down to follow up on ones that are found. Figure B.1 is more relevant to careful, bottom-up, module-by-module testing. PSOT contains numerous testing functions of this type, although they are unobtrusively located.

Figure B.2 shows another example of how a specification model can provide useful information. It shows parametric testing of the algorithm for the Primary Factors methodology. To illustrate its interpretation, note that if the primary and secondary values are 8 and 8, respectively, then the score will be 10—the primary value plus the maximum adjustment. If the primary two influences were, say, –10 and 8, respectively, the result would be –8.4. This was

Figure B.1
An Illustrative Diagnostics Array for Verification Testing

Sample of Diagnostic for Cost Calculations (All Models)

Iteration (Run)	1
Personal Risks, Opportunity Costs Q	Very Low
Countervailing Social Costs Q	Very Low
Intimidation (+) by Government Q	Very Low
Intimidation (-) by Insurgents Q	Very High
Intimidation (-) weight	0.3
Fear of Government Victory	Very Low
Fear of Insurgent Victory	Very Low
Weight of Feared Insurgent Victory	0.8
Adjustment	2
Costs Threshold for TLWS Q	Medium
Predominance Parameter	0.3

Diagnostic for Costs ▾ ☐ Totals

Comparison of Costs Results Factors ▾ ☐ Totals

	LWS	PF	PF Sto
Personal Risks	1	1	1
Countervailing Costs	1	1	1
Intim. by Govt.	1	1	1
Intim by Insurgents	9	9	9
Agg. Intim.	-7.1	-7.1	-7
Fear govt. victory	1	1	1
Fear Insurgent victory	1	1	1
Agg. victory	-0.9	-0.9	0.9
Primary Costs Factor		Intimidation	Intimidation
Secondary Costs Factor		Personal Risks and Opportunity Costs	Personal Risks and Opportunity Costs
Primary Cost		-7.1	-7
Secondary Cost		1	1
Ratio of Weights		1	1
Costs	-7.1	-6.9	-6.8
Accept of Costs	1	1	1

RAND *TR1220-B.1*

Figure B.2
An Example of Verification Testing as Part of Model Documentation

Mid Value of Test of PF

RW Test: 1

Adj_test: 2

Ptest ▾ ☐ Totals

Stest ▾ ☐ Totals

	-10	-8	-6	-4	-2	0	2	4	6	8	10
-10	-10	-10	-10	-10	-10	-10	-9.6	-9.2	-8.8	-8.4	-8
-8	-10	-9.6	-9.2	-8.8	-8.4	-8	-7.6	-7.2	-6.8	-6.4	-6
-6	-8	-7.6	-7.2	-6.8	-6.4	-6	-5.6	-5.2	-4.8	-4.4	-4
-4	-6	-5.6	-5.2	-4.8	-4.4	-4	-3.6	-3.2	-2.8	-2.4	-2
-2	-4	-3.6	-3.2	-2.8	-2.4	-2	-1.6	-1.2	-0.8	-0.4	0
0	-2	-2	-2	-2	-2	0	0.4	0.8	1.2	1.6	2
2	0	0	0	0	0	2	2.4	2.8	3.2	3.6	4
4	2	2	2	2	2	4	4.4	4.8	5.2	5.6	6
6	4	4	4	4	4	6	6.4	6.8	7.2	7.6	8
8	6	6	6	6	6	8	8.4	8.8	9.2	9.6	10
10	8	8	8	8	8	10	10	10	10	10	10

RAND *TR1220-B.1*

the type of behavior intended as an implementation of the belief that the first factor should dominate and the second influence results on the margin.

Validation

Model validation has been discussed in dozens of papers and reports (Ritchie, 1992; Youngblood et al., 2000; Balci, 2001; Balci et al., 2011; Hartley, 2010). It is especially difficult for models, including social-science models, that are beset with uncertainties (Bigelow and Davis, 2003). These cannot be validated classically by comparing model predictions against reality in controlled experiments. Special challenges also arise in connection with distributed simulation and the dream of model composability. The modules to be composed must not only "connect" and run (an issue only of adopting agreed syntaxes), but must also make sense substantively. Substantive validity is often undercut by deeply buried or implicit assumptions that were reasonable when a module was built, with one context in mind, but are not reasonable for the new context (Davis and Anderson, 2003; Davis and Anderson, 2004; National Research Council, 2006). Considerable effort is needed in multi-modeling to assure reasonableness, as discussed well in Louie and Carley (2008).

The feasibility of substantive composition is much enhanced by comprehensibility and transparency features too often absent when dealing with complex computer programs that have no separate and understandable conceptual model that can be assessed by subject-area specialists without the additional issues of understanding implementation in a computer program. The importance of separating model (conceptual model) from program was emphasized by such pioneers as Richard Nance (Nance, 1999), Robert Sargent (Sargent, 2010), Osman Balci (Balci et al., 2011), and Bernard Zeigler (Zeigler, 1984). The distinction broke down over the past two decades as personal computers have made it more natural to design, build, and experiment with models by simultaneously designing and programming. We believe, however, that such problems are greatly mitigated by building separately reviewable modules, documenting the essence of the conceptual models in mathematical and logical terms, and using a high-level programming language that is reasonably self-documenting to specify the rest of the details—taking care to structure the program around the model rather than around implantation-specific issues. This reasoning helped to motivate the approach of this report.

APPENDIX C

Eliciting Factor Values

A practical question in using this report's model with subject-matter experts is how to elicit estimates of factors efficiently. Some experts will make such estimates directly and quickly, with their estimates aligning closely with the intent of the model. In other cases, however, it will not be so easy. For example, if asked whether insurgent activities are low, medium, or high, an expert might say high because of there being a sizable number of monthly incidents. On what basis, however, would ten incidents per month be regarded as low, medium, or high? Comparison with the pre-insurgency norm? Comparison with other insurgencies? Further, how do we assure that the qualitative values of different factors are in some sense being measured on the same scale?

For the purpose of causal modeling, we are interested in knowing whether the factor in question can potentially have a large effect on higher-level phenomena, such as the likelihood of widespread revolution.

To illustrate, consider a trivial factor tree as in Figure C.1. Suppose that we are interested in assessing D by using a model that combines A, B, and C. In trying to elicit an estimate of C from an expert, we actually want to know the estimated effect of C for each of the various possible values of A and B. The expert being consulted, however, may already have a sense (but not necessarily an expert sense) of A's and B's values. Will that implicitly affect his characterization of C? We would prefer not, so that we can exercise the model with different assumptions about A and B.

The problem would be nonexistent if the phenomenon were linear, if D were just a sum of effects from A, B, and C. That, however, is not the reality. For example, the effect of the acceptability of costs and risks would be zero if there were no insurgency to support, but might be quite high if organizational effectiveness and motivation were significant. We do not want the elicited value of C to reflect these effects of A and B.

Figure C.1
A Trivial Factor Tree

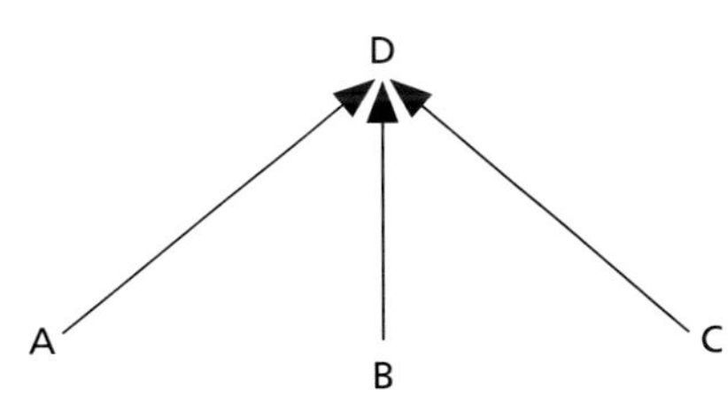

RAND *TR1220-C.1*

In expert elicitation, it is important to ask the minimum number of questions needed to obtain key information. Table C.1 illustrates our approach for the factor tree of Figure C.1 in cases in which more elaboration is necessary. The question assumes that A, B, and C have threshold values of Medium.

> *We are interested in estimating D, which is affected by A, B, and C. Assume that A and B have at least medium effects on D (i.e., they are not limiting). Now, as the expert on C, please answer two questions:*
>
> 1. *Is C so small as to be limiting, so as to make D small? Please answer Yes, Maybe, or No.*
> 2. *If not, that is, if C is not limiting, is C large enough to have a big effect on D? Again, please answer Yes, Maybe, or No.*

This formulation focuses the expert on effects, rather than factor-idiosyncratic "natural" scales, reduces the ambiguity of the expert's answers, and allows us to extrapolate to questions not asked.

Table C.1 shows the mapping we use in interpreting responses to the two questions. The last column explains the rationale for the value of C inferred.

Table C.1
Mapping of Responses to Scores

Answer to Question 1	Answer to Question 2	Value of C Inferred	Rationale
Yes	—	1	Literal interpretation
Maybe	No	3	(1/2)2+(1/2)(5), rounded down
Maybe	Maybe	5	(1/2)(2)+(1/2)(7.5), rounded
Maybe	Yes	5	(1/2)(2)+(1/2)(9), rounded down
No	No	5	Literal interpretation
No	Maybe	7	Average of 5 and 9
No	Yes	9	Literal interpretation

APPENDIX D

Mathematics for "And" and "Or" Relationships

Introduction

This appendix elaborates on combining relationships indicated by "~ands" and "ors" in factor trees. Philosophically, the actual social-science phenomena being modeled should be the primary concern, with mathematics serving rather than leading. Thus, discussion first distinguishes classes of behaviors. Subsequent sections then describe suitable approximate mathematics: First, we give simplified discussions assuming only two factors (variables) A and B that combine for an effect E; we then generalize with vector-array mathematics.* The result is an initial set of building-block tools to represent behaviors that are the result of factors combining in simple ways to counter, reinforce, or dilute each others' effects. Much more complicated relationships are, of course, possible.

The scope and assumptions for the approach are as follows, using the simple instance of two factors A and B to explain. They apply also when more factors are treated.

1. *Signs and Ranges.* A and B may be of opposite sign, in which case their influences counter each other. A, B, and E are constrained to the range –10 to 10 inclusive, denoted [–10,10].
2. *Weights.* A and B have normalized relative weights W_A and W_B.
3. *Probabilities.* A and B may be probability distributions reflecting uncertainty about facts or underlying stochastic processes.
4. *Order Independence.* The function $E(A,B)$ is assumed to be independent of the order in which A and B are considered or the order in which information on their values arrives.
5. *Simple Combining Relationships.* $E(A,B)$ is assumed to have one of a few specified simple, stepwise-linear forms.

The first three items use the word "may" because A and B will often be of the same sign, have equal weights, and be deterministic. The fourth item, on order dependence, is significant because individual and social real-life behaviors sometimes depend on history and the order of stimuli, as with the notorious decisionmaker who always accepts suggestions of the last adviser to see him.† The last item represents our attempt to go as far as possible with simple building-

* Arrays are n-dimensional generalizations of vectors (one dimension) and matrices (two dimensions). Theoretical physicists often use the term "tensor."

† If understood and reliable, order dependence can be represented by defining A as the first stimulus and B as the second. If order is unknown, a stochastic formulation could be used or both cases evaluated. If order dependence were ephemeral, focus could be on the end result—by analogy to an economist's equilibrium solution. In what follows, we do not consider such complications.

block forms. Real-world combining relationships are not linear, but much can be done with step-wise linear approximations.

We now proceed by asking a series of questions to distinguish among cases; we then provide corresponding analytical representations.

Basic Questions and Cases

Are All Factors Required (Nonlinearity), or Can Factors Substitute?

Simplified Discussion

If an effect or behavior E depends on *both* A and B having at least threshold values A_0 and B_0, we denote that with a connector arc labeled "~ands," (Figure D.1). In this case, A and B are not substitutable, and $E(A,B)$ is nonlinear.

The "~" indicates "approximate" because when such "and" relationships are asserted, exceptions usually exist. The notation is motivated by simple logic where, if E, A, and B are true-false (1-0) propositions, then the expression $E = (A \text{ and } B) = (A \wedge B)$ implies that E is true only if both A and B are true. For more general cases, A, B, and E can have a range of values, it is natural to use the relationship below. As a starting point, it assumes that A, B, and E are non-negative and that the variables and their thresholds have the same sign, as assured by requiring that the products AA_0 and BB_0 are non-negative.

$$\begin{array}{l} \text{For } A \geq 0,\ B \geq 0,\ AA_0 \geq 0, \text{ and } BB_0 \geq 0 \\ \text{If } A \geq A_0 \text{ and } B \geq B_0 \\ \text{Then } E = E(A,B) \\ \text{Else } 0 \end{array} \qquad \text{Eq. D.1}$$

This does not say what the functional relationship $E(A,B)$ is when both A and B meet or exceed thresholds. That is considered below.

Equation D.1 is equivalent to

$$\begin{array}{l} \text{For } A \geq 0,\ B \geq 0,\ AA_0 \geq 0, \text{ and } BB_0 \geq 0 \\ \text{If } A < A_0 \text{ or } B < B_0 \\ \text{Then } 0 \\ \text{Else } E = E(A,B). \end{array} \qquad \text{Eq. D.2}$$

That is, an "and" relationship can be expressed with an "or" relationship.

Figure D.1
Simple "And" Relationship

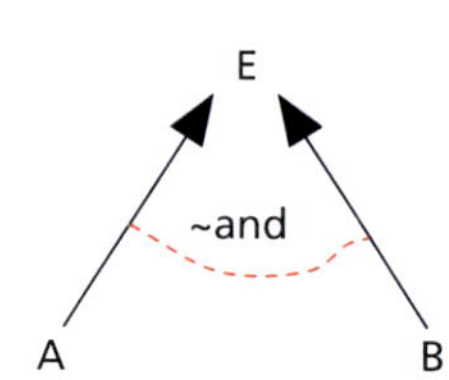

RAND *TR1220-D.1*

This type of combining rule is often appropriate. Any system with two critical factors will, by definition, fail unless both are adequately effective. A military fighter aircraft is useless if it has everything else but not weapons. An effective organization must have adequate resources, not just leadership.

Generalization

A, B, and *E* may be negative, in which case a more general expression is

$$\begin{aligned}&\text{For } AA_0 \geq 0 \text{ and } BB_0 \geq 0\\&\text{If } |A| < |A_0| \text{ or } |B| < |B_0|\\&\text{Then } 0\\&\text{Else } E = E(A,B).\end{aligned} \qquad \text{Eq. D.3}$$

Also, if instead of two scalar variables *A* and *B*, we had a vector with elements **A**, **B**, **C** . . ., the condition would be*

$$\begin{aligned}&\text{For } \mathbf{FF}_0 \geq 0 \text{ (all components, for consistency of signs)}\\&\text{If } |\mathbf{F}| - |\mathbf{F}^0| < 0\\&\text{Then } E = 0\\&\text{Else } E = E(\mathbf{F}).\end{aligned} \qquad \text{Eq. D.4}$$

Suppose next that both *A* and *B* (or, more generally, all elements of **F**) are at or above threshold values. What next? How do they combine?

Does the Effect Depend More on Largest Factors or on Averages?

In looking at factor trees for a number of applications, we concluded that it is necessary to distinguish among cases where *A* and *B* can counter, reinforce, or dilute each other's effects. Factors of different sign naturally counter each other, but reinforcement versus dilution is less clear. For example, if *A* and *B* are 5 and 4, should *E* be more like 9, or at least something greater than 5 (reinforcement), or should it instead be 4.5, the average? If *A* and *B* are 8 and 2, should *E* be more like 8 or more like 5?

Both relationships exist in reality. For example, we may be effectively motivated by the strongest of the possible contributing motivations, with perhaps some reinforcement by another. In contrast, organizational effectiveness is likely to be more of a weighted average over such contributors as leadership, management, ideological package, and resources. Our assertions could be empirically tested, but the reader will presumably agree with the examples. Such rough-cut distinctions leave much unspecified, which we discuss below more rigorously.

A Minimum Set of Simple Combining Rules

Based on the questions of the last section, at least three combining rules (methods) are needed. All can be nonlinear, but they break into piece-wise linear forms. We call the three meth-

---

* The first line is implemented in Analytica as, e.g., If Min ($\mathbf{F}^*\mathbf{F}^0$, index) < 0 Then "Sign Error" Else, which means that if any of the elements of the product vector are negative, it implies a sign error. Implementation would be slightly different in other languages.

ods Primary Factors (PF), Thresholded Linear Weighted Sums (TLWS), and TLWS Variant (TLWSV).

Primary Factors

The Primary Factors method represents countering (by opposite sign) and reinforcement. Let us begin with a simplified description and then generalize.

Simplified Representation

If A is larger than B, both are positive, and they combine for effect E, then E is given in the PF method by

$$\begin{aligned}&\text{For } A, B, \text{ and } \Delta \text{ non-negative}\\&E = MIN[A + B\Delta, A + \Delta]\\&\text{(constrained to } [-10,10]).\end{aligned} \qquad \text{Eq. D.5}$$

That is, the effect E is the value of the primary factor plus a correction, which grows with B, but cannot be greater than Δ. Logically, we also want the correction to be smaller for small A than for large A because we wouldn't want the case of a 3 and 3 (A and B both 3) to generate, say, 6. That is, if both A and B are weak influences, the result should still be weak (another empirically testable assertion). A simple algorithm accomplishing this is

$$\Delta = \frac{|A|}{10}\Delta_{max}\,. \qquad \text{Eq. D.6}$$

Here, Δ_{max} is a constant chosen by the user familiar with how A and B combine. The "right" value, of course, is an empirical matter, but our implementation of PSOT uses a default of 2 so that the reinforcement effect is relatively small.

Combining Equations D.5 and D.6 yields

$$\begin{aligned}&\text{For } A, B, \text{ and } \Delta_{max} \text{ non-negative}\\&E = MIN[A + \frac{B}{10}\Delta_{max}, A + \Delta_{max}]\\&\text{(constrained to } [-10,10]).\end{aligned} \qquad \text{Eq. D.7}$$

Generalization

Figure D.2 shows our intent for cases that allow positive and negative values. It assumes that $|W_A A| \geq |W_B B|$ and that weights are equal. Although drawn for a particular value of $|A|$, the generalization should be clear: E either increases or decreases with B, but the magnitude of corrections can be no more than Δ, which varies with $|A|$ as in Eq. D.6.

Since the purely mathematical way of expressing such things is messy, pseudo code is usually convenient, but—since Analytica is a high-level language with syntax that often looks like pseudo code—we show the Analytica code generating E in Figure D.3. The first line restricts E

Figure D.2
Four Cases for Primary Factors Calculation

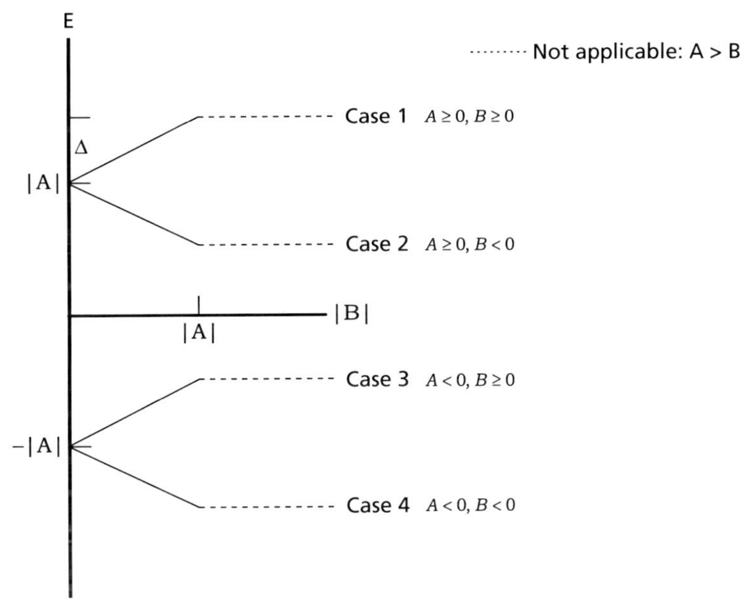

RAND *TR1220-D.2*

Note: This assumes equal weights for *A* and *B*.

to be in [–10,10], i.e., between –10 and 10. This also allows for different weights. The variable *RW* is

$$\frac{W_B}{W_A},$$

the ratio of weights for *A* and *B*. The last line checks against divisions by zero as a guard against inappropriate inputs or other errors.

Singularity. A complication in rigorously specifying the combining rule is dealing with the singularity where *A* and *B* are equal but have opposite signs, as illustrated in Figure D.4. The singularity is troublesome since if *A* and *B* are almost equal but opposite in signs, a small change of assessment in either could reverse which is primary, changing the calculated value of *E* from, say, 8 to –8 (due to *A* being almost 10, *B* being –10, and the maximum correction having a magnitude of 2).

This type of difficulty is common when using discretized mathematics and thresholds. We provide two alternative resolutions of this singular case:

- Have the model report "Tie" if *A* and *B* are "close" in absolute value (e.g., within 1 on a –10 to 10 scale)
- Have the model report the average between the values that would be obtained depending on whether *A* or *B* is primary.

Figure D.3
Algorithm Generating Result *E* for Primary Factors Method

```
Constrain_range1010(
If A ≥ 0 and B ≥ 0
Then
   If B ≤ 10/(RW + .001)
   Then A +Δmax × B × RW/10
   Else A + Δmax
Else
   If A ≥ 0 and B < 0
   Then
      If B ≥ –(10/(RW + .001))
      Then A + Δmax × B × RW/10
      Else A – Δmax
   Else
      If A < 0 and B ≥ 0
      Then
         If B ≤ 10/(RW + .001)
         Then A + Δmax × B × RW/10
         Else A + Δmax
      Else
         If A < 0 and B < 0
         Then
            If B ≥ –(10/(RW + .001))
            Then A + Δmax × B × RW/10
            Else A – Δmax
         Else "Error")
```

The first of these is preferred and implemented in our Analytica prototype, but in other languages charting software might react badly to "tie," in which case the second option could be used.

Thresholded Linear Weighted Sums and Its Variant

Simplified Discussion

The second and third methods (TLWS and TLWSV) correspond to averaging with some constraints. These can represent countering, reinforcement, and dilution. Averaging is accomplished with a thresholded linear weighted sum. Given threshold effects, however, what happens at and below threshold? The answer depends on whether B (the smaller factor) either (1) matters only if it reaches threshold or (2) always matters.

To explain these two cases, suppose first that someone is evaluating the desirability of a course of action. He might have a long list of potential benefits, but—if he sees no basis for some of them, he will probably discard further consideration of them. Or, if assessing risks, he

Figure D.4
Approximation at Discontinuity

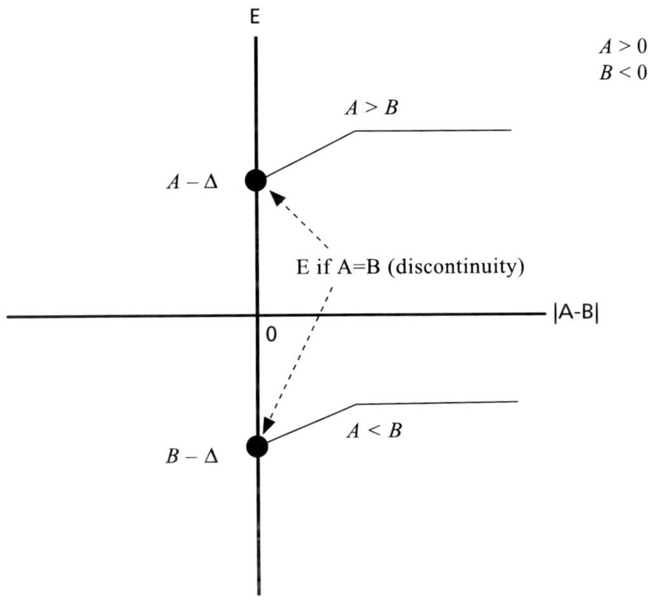

RAND *TR1220-D.4*

will probably ignore classes of risk for which he sees no evidence or to which he is psychologically insensitive. All of us ignore sub-threshold risks routinely.

Next suppose that a factor in question, B, represents something like a risk about which the person or group always worries—even if there is no immediate evidence of B being significant. For potential insurgency supporters, there might *always* be a perceived risk of severe government repression, even if the government has so far shown no inclinations in that direction. Or, to use a more everyday example, a wise investor with a sense of history will worry about having at least some of his portfolio in extremely safe instruments, such as government bonds, even if the economy is doing well with no dark clouds evident.

The mathematics for these two methods is easily expressed. In the trivial case of two factors A and B, both positive, the usual linear weighted sum would be

$$E = W_A A + W_B B. \qquad \text{Eq. D.8}$$

If the factors matter only if above threshold, and B is below threshold, then

$$E = A. \qquad \text{Eq. D.9}$$

The result is A rather than $W_A A$ because, if B is irrelevant, it has no weight and the weight of A is 1. This is what we refer to as TLWS. If, however, B is always a consideration, the behavior is better represented by but using either 0 or some B_0 instead of B if B is below threshold. We call this TLWSV, the variant method.

Generalization

For a more general expressions of these two rules, consider $\mathbf{F^0}$ to be a vector of factors, which may be positive, negative or zero. The superscript "0" indicates that this is the initial vector before thresholding. Let **T** be the corresponding vector of threshold values and $\mathbf{W^0}$ be the vector of initial weights. If the thresholds were all 0, then the result of combining the factors would be E, given by standard linear weighted sums:

$$\begin{aligned}&\text{For } \mathbf{W}^0 \geq 0 \text{ and } \mathbf{FF}^0 \geq 0 \text{ (consistency of signs)},\\ &E = \mathbf{W}^0 \bullet \mathbf{F}^0 = \sum_{i=1}^{n} W_i^0 F_i^0\\ &\text{(constrained to } [-10,10]).\end{aligned} \qquad \text{Eq. D.10}$$

The concept of thresholded linear weighted sums is that we compute the result as a scalar (dot) product but replace sub-threshold values of $\mathbf{F^0}$. If we do so, however, two issues arise: With what do we replace them and do we still sum over all variables?

If the Factors Matter Only When Above Threshold. If a given variable (factor) matters only if it is at or above threshold (in absolute-value terms), then we discard the factor and perform the average with the remaining variables. To do so, however, requires renormalization of weights. To write the mathematics it is convenient to define a "delta function" **D**(**X**). **X** can be any expression that can be evaluated as either true or false, i.e., as 1 or 0. Thus, it can be a vector or a vector of true-false tests.

$$\begin{aligned}&\mathbf{D}(\mathbf{X}):\\ &\text{If } \mathbf{X} \geq 0 \text{ Then 1 Else 0.}\end{aligned} \qquad \text{Eq. D.11}$$

Using the notation that $\boldsymbol{XY}$ is a simple vector multiplication such that the i-th element of the resulting vector is $\mathbf{X}_i\mathbf{Y}_i$, we then have for the TLWS method:

$$\begin{aligned}&\text{TLWS Method:}\\ &\text{For } \mathbf{F}^0\mathbf{T} \geq 0 \text{ (all elements; consistency of signs)}\\ &\mathbf{F} \equiv \mathbf{F}^0\mathbf{D}(|\mathbf{F}| - |\mathbf{T}| \geq 0)\\ &\mathbf{W} \equiv \mathbf{W}^0\mathbf{D}(|\mathbf{F}| - |\mathbf{T}| \geq 0)\\ &\mathbf{W}^r \equiv \frac{\mathbf{W}}{\mathbf{W} \bullet \mathbf{I}^T} = \frac{\mathbf{W}}{\sum_{i=1}^{n} W_i}\\ &E = \mathbf{W}^r \bullet \mathbf{F} = \sum_{i=1}^{n} \frac{W_j F_j}{\sum_{j=1}^{n} W_j}\\ &\text{(constrained to } [-10,10]).\end{aligned} \qquad \text{Eq. D.12}$$

The modified vector **F** is the original except that its below-threshold elements are set to 0. The modified weighting vector **W** replaces the original weights of below-threshold factors with 0. $\mathbf{W}^r$ is the vector of renormalized weights.* The last line expresses E as a scalar product, as with normal linear weighted sums, except that the modified vectors are used to represent thresholding. Note that is valid independent of whether the factors in **F** are positive, negative, or a mixture.

If the Factors Always Matter (TLWS Variant, TLWSV). The generalization of the TLWSV cases is ultimately similar. The vector **F** is the same as $\mathbf{F^0}$ except that below-threshold elements are replaced by *either* 0 or the element's threshold value, while the vector of weights **W** is the same as the original rather than a renormalized version. The corresponding general equations are as follows. We need a variant of the delta function that includes the option to substitute either 0 or the threshold value (deciding separately for each element of the relevant vector), so we define it as **D2**:

$$\begin{aligned}&\mathbf{D2}(\mathbf{X}, \mathrm{T}; \mathbf{p}):\\&\text{If } \mathbf{X} \geq 0 \text{ Then } 1\\&\text{Else If } \mathbf{p} = 1 \text{ Then } 0 \text{ Else } \mathbf{T}.\end{aligned} \qquad \text{Eq. D.13}$$

As in Eq. D.12, we can then write the equations to obtain:

TLWSV (Variant) Method:

For $\mathbf{F}^0\mathbf{T} \geq 0$, (all elements, for consistency of signs)

$$\mathbf{F} \equiv \mathbf{F}^0\mathbf{D}2(\left|\mathbf{F}^0\right| \geq |\mathbf{T}|, \mathbf{T}, \mathbf{p} = 1) \qquad \text{Eq. D.14}$$

$$E = \mathbf{W}^0 \bullet \mathbf{F}(\mathbf{p}) = \sum_{i=1}^{n} W_i^0 F_i(p_i).$$

The Hybrid Case. We might want to treat some elements of the vector $\mathbf{F^0}$ as always mattering and others as mattering only if above thresholds. Further, we might want to set some of the former to 0 when below threshold and some to their threshold values.

One way to accomplish this is shown in Equation D.15, which defines a vector **Q** to have elements of 1 if the element matters only if the element reaches threshold and 0 if it always matters. This allows calculating a revised weighting vector that replaces the sub-threshold elements' weight with 0 (third line) for elements having **Q** values of 1. The other weights are unchanged. However, we now need renormalized weights $\mathbf{W}^r$. The vector of thresholded factors **F** is calculated as above, in Equation D.14. Finally, the effect E is the scalar product of $\mathbf{W}^r$ and **F**. This result is general, covering instances in which the elements of **F** have arbitrary sign. Each element i can be treated as relevant only if at or above threshold ($Q_i = 1$), or can be treated as always relevant ($Q_i = 0$), in which case the sub-threshold value may be set to 0 ($p = 1$) or the threshold value ($p = 0$).

* Scalar, inner, or dot products are represented with different syntaxes depending on computer language. In Analytica, the scalar product of vectors **W** and **F** is represented by "Sum (W, F, I)", where I is the name of the index over which the sum is to be performed. Specifying index is necessary because **W** and **B** may be n-dimensional arrays because of distinguishing between, say, region, year, tribe, or value of an uncertain parameter. Other languages represent scalar products with For loops or other such devices.

General for TLWS and TLWSV:

If $\mathbf{F}^0\mathbf{T} \geq 0$, (all elements, for consistency of signs)

$$\mathbf{W}^1 \equiv (1-\mathbf{Q})\mathbf{W}^0 + \mathbf{Q}\mathbf{W}^0\mathbf{Delta}(|\mathbf{F}^0| - |\mathbf{T}| \geq 0)$$

$$\mathbf{W}^r \equiv \frac{\mathbf{W}^1}{\mathbf{W}^1 \bullet \mathbf{I}^T} \qquad \text{Eq. D.15}$$

$$\mathbf{F(p)} \equiv \mathrm{D2}(|\mathbf{F}| - |\mathbf{T}|) \geq 0; \mathbf{T}; \mathbf{p})$$

$$E = \mathbf{W}^r \bullet \mathbf{F(p)}$$

(Constrain to $[-10,10]$).

Example

The reader may wish to work through this manually for an illustrative case. If so, consider the case of three factors *A*, *B*, and *C* with corresponding thresholds *a*, *b*, and *c*, and with initial weights W_a, W_b, and W_c, which are all equal (and, hence, 1/3). Suppose that *A* is relevant only for $A \geq a$, but that *B* and *C* are always relevant. Suppose that *B* uses a sub-threshold value of 0 ($p = 1$) and *C* a sub-threshold value of *c* ($p = 0$). Thus,

$$\mathbf{F^0} = \{A,B,C\}$$
$$\mathbf{T} = \{\mathrm{a, b, c}\}$$
$$\mathbf{W^0} = \{W_\mathrm{a}, W_\mathrm{b}, W_\mathrm{c}\}.$$

For all three factors below their thresholds, we have, according to Eq. D.15, that

$$\mathbf{F} = \{0,0,\mathrm{c}\}$$
$$\mathbf{W^r} = \{0, 1/2, 1/2\}$$
$$E = \mathrm{c}/2.$$

Deciding on the Combining Rule

Figure D.5 shows how to decide on the combing rule using a decision tree format. The idea, when implementing each combining relationship of a model based on a factor tree, is to ask the various questions indicated and decide on the rule/algorithm. In implementing PSOT, we concluded that motivation for public support could be substantial even if some or many of the possible contributors to motivation were small. Thus, we went down the right half of the figure. We then concluded that motivation is typically determined by the primary potential source of motivation, rather than by some average. Thus, we arrived at the Primary Factors approach at node 3.

In considering Acceptability of Costs, we again did not see that an "and" condition was appropriate, so we went down the right side of the tree. We concluded that a case could be made for any of the three possibilities (3)–(5), depending on context.

Much the same information is presented in tabular form in Table D.1, but with numerical examples in the left column and some additional detail.

Figure D.5
Deciding on the Combining-Rule Algorithm

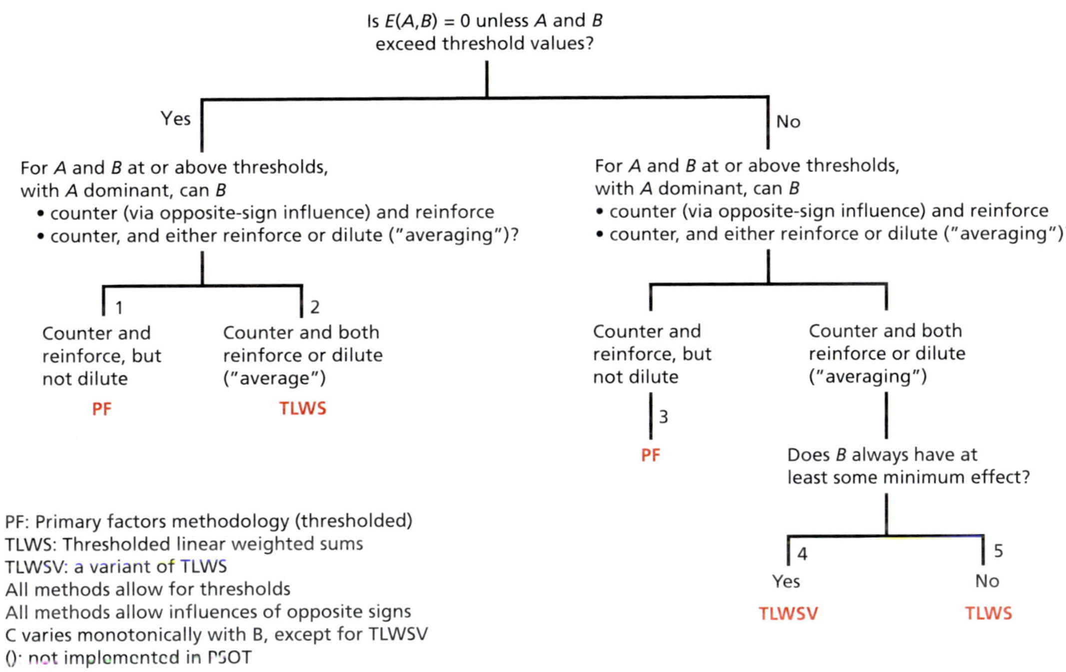

RAND *TR1220-D.5*

Adjustments, Enhancements, and Limitations

The PF, TLWS, and TLWSV methods include several parameters by which behavior of the combining relationships can be tuned. These include thresholds, the extent of the maximum correction in PF methodology, the slope of change in that methodology, and some other detailed features. Additional embellishments are possible. These include:

1. Extending the PF methodology to allow for more than just the second-largest influence to affect the result.
2. Allowing for selected additional types of nonlinearity and interconnectedness.

It is unclear whether further enhancements would make sense or whether a different approach would then be more suitable. For example, if one believed that the phenomena were appropriately described with Bayesian-net mathematics in which the nodes of a tree are probabilities, then the built-in features of a tool such as Netica or Genie might suffice. If interdependencies were especially important, then a Systems Dynamic model might prove better. If combining relationships involved, say, trigonometric functions, as with $E = A \, Sin \, (B)$, then nothing like the PF, TLWS, or TLWSV methods would make sense. This said, the three building blocks appear to have considerable potential.

Table D.1
Choosing the Combining-Rule Method

	B Always Matters			B Only Matters if Above Threshold		
Behavior Desired	**PF**	**TLWS**	**TLWSV**	**PF**	**TLWS**	**TLWSV**
Reinforce or counter primary (with positive and negative influences); do not dilute by averaging across same-sign influences[1] 9,–8 → 8.2 9,5 → 9.3 8, 7 → 8 7	••••			••••		
Reinforce or counter primary (with positive and negative influences) *and* dilute primary on margin with secondary of same sign[1] 9,–8 → 8.2 9, 5 → 9.3 8,7 → 8.7	••••			••••		
Assess net effect from positive and negative, small and large influences via weighted sums 9, –8 → 5 [on the 0–10 scale] 9, 5 → 7 8,7 → 7.5		••••				••••
Features						
B for B < B_0	0	0	B_0	0	0	NA
Monotonicity	Yes[2]	Yes	Yes	Yes[2]	Only for no-threshold case[3]	Yes
Terms for net assessment (if A has *n* elements)		*n*	*n*		*n* – 1	*n* – 1

NOTE: The notation •••• indicates that a method was a primary method used.

[1] Examples refer to values of A and B, and the result intended. They assume a B threshold of 5, equal weights, and a PF maximum adjustment of 2.

[2] A discontinuity occurs if A = B.

[3] If B's value moves above threshold slightly, this increases the number of terms in and almost necessarily reduces the value of the net assessment; the assessment then increases with further increases in B, creating an inherent non-monotonicity.

Bibliography

Balci, Osman (2001), "Verification, Validation, and Accreditation Recommended Practices Guide," edited by Defense Modeling and Simulation Office.

Balci, Osman, James D. Arthur, and William F. Ormsby (2011), "Achieving Reusability and Composability with a Simulation Conceptual Model," *Journal of Simulation*, 5, 157–165.

Bankes, Steven C. (1993), "Exploratory Modeling for Policy Analysis," *Operations Research*, 41, 435–449.

Bigelow, James H., and Paul K. Davis (2003), *Implications for Model Validation of Multiresolution, Multiperspective Modeling (MRMPM) and Exploratory Analysis,* Santa Monica, Calif.: RAND Corporation. As of June 10, 2012:
http://www.rand.org/pubs/monograph_reports/MR1750.html

Bjorgo, Tore, and John Horgan (2009), *Leaving Terrorism Behind: Disengagement from Political Violence*, New York: Routledge.

Body, Howard, and Colin Marston (2011), "The Peace Support Operations Model: Origin, Development, Philosophy and Use," *Journal of Defense Modeling and Simulation*, 8, 69–77.

Briscoe, Erica, et al. (2011), "Closing the Micro-Macro Divide in Modeling Technology Adoption," in *Proceedings of 2nd Annual Conference of the Computational Social Science Society of America, Sante Fe, New Mexico*. As of December 10, 2012:
http://www.gtri.gatech.edu/files/media/Briscoe_CSSSA_Macro_Micro4.pdf

Bueno de Mesquita, Bruce (1983), *The War Trap*, New Haven, Conn.: Yale University Press.

——— (2009), *The Practitioner's Game: Using the Logic of Brazen Self-Interest to See and Shape the Future*, New York: Random House.

Carley, Kathleen M. (2012), "Deterrence Modeling Using Dynamic Network Analysis, presented at a special meeting of the Military Operations Research Society (MORS), March 19–22, 2012," unpublished briefing, Pittsburgh: Carnegie Mellon University, Center for Computational Analysis of Social and Organizational Systems.

Carley, Kathleen M., and Terrill Frantz (2009), "Modeling Organizational and Individual Decision Making," in *Handbook of Systems Engineering and Management*, edited by Andrew P. Sage and William B. Rouse, New York: Wiley, 723–762.

Center for Computational Analysis of Social and Organizational Systems, homepage, no date. As of December 7, 2012:
http://www.casos.cs.cmu.edu/

Davis, Paul K (ed.) (1994), *New Challenges in Defense Planning: Rethinking How Much is Enough*, Santa Monica, Calif.: RAND Corporation. As of June 10, 2012:
http://www.rand.org/pubs/monograph_reports/MR400.html

——— (2002), *Analytic Architecture for Capabilities-Based Planning, Mission-System Analysis, and Transformation*, Santa Monica, Calif.: RAND Corporation. As of January 30, 2013:
http://www.rand.org/pubs/monograph_reports/MR1513.html

——— (2003a), "Exploratory Analysis and Implications for Modeling," in Stuart E. Johnson, Martin C. Libicki, and Greg F. Treverton, eds., *New Challenges, New Tools for Defense Decisionmaking*, Santa Monica, Calif: RAND, pp. 255–283. As of January 30, 2013:
http://www.rand.org/pubs/monograph_reports/MR1576.html

——— (2003b), "Synthetic Cognitive Modeling of Adversaries for Effects-Based Planning," *Proceedings of the SPIE*, 4716, 2002, 236–250. Reprinted in Kulick and Davis (2003).

——— (2006), "A Qualitative Multiresolution Model for Counterterrorism," *Proceedings of the SPIE*, Vol. 62270F.

——— (2009a), "Representing Social Science Knowledge Analytically," in *Social Science for Counterterrorism: Putting the Pieces Together*, edited by Paul K. Davis and Kim Cragin, Santa Monica, Calif.: RAND Corporation, 401–452.

——— (2009b), "Specifying the Content of Humble Social-Science Models," *Proceedings of the 2009 Summer Computer Simulation Conference*, Istanbul, reprinted by RAND. As of January 30, 2013:
http://www.rand.org/pubs/reprints/RP1408-1.html

——— (2011), "Primer for Building Factor Trees to Represent Social-Science Knowledge," *Proceedings of the 2011 Winter Simulation Conference* (included here as Appendix A).

——— (2012a), *Influencing Violent Extremist Organizations and Their Supporters Without Adverse Side Effects,* Santa Monica, Calif.: RAND Corporation, working draft. As of June 10:
http://www.rand.org/pubs/working_papers/WR909.html

——— (2012b), *Lessons from RAND's Work on Planning Under Uncertainty for National Security,* Santa Monica Calif.: RAND Corporation. As of December 10, 2012:
http://www.rand.org/pubs/technical_reports/TR1249.html

——— (ed.) (2011), *Dilemmas of Intervention: Social Science for Stabilization and Reconstruction*, Santa Monica, Calif.: RAND Corporation. As of June 10, 2012:
http://www.rand.org/pubs/monographs/MG1119.html

Davis, Paul K., and Robert H. Anderson (2003), *Improving the Composability of Department of Defense Models and Simulations*, Santa Monica, Calif.: RAND Corporation. As of June 10, 2012:
http://www.rand.org/pubs/monographs/MG101.html

——— (2004), "Improving the Composability of DoD Models and Simulations," *Journal of Defense Modeling and Simulation*, 1, 24–36.

Davis, Paul K., Steven C. Bankes, and Michael Egner (2007), *Enhancing Strategic Planning with Massive Scenario Generation: Theory and Experiments,* Santa Monica, Calif.: RAND Corporation. As of June 10, 2012:
http://www.rand.org/pubs/technical_reports/TR392.html

Davis, Paul K., and James H. Bigelow (1998), *Experiments in Multiresolution Modeling (MRM),* Santa Monica, Calif.: RAND Corporation. As of June 10, 2012:
http://www.rand.org/pubs/monograph_reports/MR1004.html

Davis, Paul K., and Kim Cragin (eds.) (2009), *Social Science for Counterterrorism: Putting the Pieces Together*, Santa Monica, Calif.: RAND Corporation, 2009. As of June 9, 2012:
http://www.rand.org/pubs/monographs/MG849.html

Davis, Paul K., Eric Larson, Zachary Haldeman, Mustafa Oguz, and Yashodhara Rana (2012), *Understanding and Influencing Public Support for Insurgency and Terrorism*, Santa Monica, Calif.: RAND Corporation. As of October 16, 2012:
http://www.rand.org/pubs/monographs/MG1122.html

Davis, Paul K., and Anastasia Norton (2011), *Structuring and Informing Decisions on Strategic Communications*, Washington, D.C.: 2010 Summer Hard Problem (SHARP), Office of the Director of National Intelligence.

Davis, Paul K., and James A. Winnefeld (1983), *the RAND Strategy Assessment Center: An Overview and Interim Conclusions About Utility and Development Options*, Santa Monica, Calif.: RAND. As of June 10, 2012:
http://www.rand.org/pubs/reports/R2945.html

Forrester, Jay W. (1963), *Industrial Dynamics*, Cambridge, Mass.: MIT Press.

George, Alexander L., and Andrew Bennett (2005), *Case Studies and Theory Development in the Social Sciences*, Cambridge, Mass.: MIT Press.

Haider, Sajiad, and Alexander H. Levis (2008), "Modeling Time-Varying Uncertain Situations Using Dynamic Influence Nets," *International Journal of Approximate Reasoning*, 49, 488–502.

Hartley, Dean (2010), "Comparing Validation Results for Two DIME/PMESII Models: Understanding Coverage Profiles," *Proceedings of the 2010 Winter Simulation Conference*, 428–440.

Helfstein, Scott (coordinator), et al. (2011), *Towards a Framework for Unintended Consequences of Influence Activities,* Washington, D.C.: Strategic Multilayer Assessment (SMA), OUSD(AT&L/DDRE), Department of Defense.

Helmus, Todd C. (2009), "Why and How Some People Become Terrorists," in *Social Science for Counterterrorism: Putting the Pieces Together*, edited by Paul K. Davis and Kim Cragin, Santa Monica, Calif.: RAND Corporation, 71–112.

Hillestad, Richard, and Paul K. Davis (2006), "GCT: Gaming Counter-Terrorism with a Two-Sided Stochastic Model for Evaluating Terrorism Strategy," Santa Monica, Calif.: RAND Corporation, unpublished.

Horgan, John (2009), *Walking Away from Terrorism (Political Violence)*, Routledge.

Howard, Ronald A., and James E. Matheson (1984), "Influence Diagrams," in *Readings on the Principles and Applications of Decision Analysis*, edited by Ronald A. Howard and James E. Matheson, Menlo Park, Calif.: Strategic Decisions Group.

——— (2005), "Influence Diagrams," *Decision Analysis*, 2, 127–144.

Jackson, Brian A. (2009), "Organizational Decisionmaking by Terrorist Groups," in *Social Science for Counterterrorism: Putting the Pieces Together*, edited by Paul K. Davis and Kim Cragin, Santa Monica, Calif.: RAND Corporation, 209–256.

Jenkins, Brian Michael (2008), *Will Terrorists Go Nuclear?* Amherst, N.Y.: Prometheus Books.

Koehler-Derrick, Gabriel (2012), "The Abbottabad Documents: Bin Laden's Cautious Strategy in Yemen," *CTC Sentinel*, May.

Kulick, Jonathan, and Paul K. Davis (2003), *Modeling Adversaries and Related Cognitive Biases*, Santa Monica, Calif.: RAND (reprints from Proceedings of the SPIE). As of June 10, 2012:
http://www.rand.org/pubs/reprints/RP1084.html

Kull, Steven, et al. (2009), "Public Opinion in the Islamic World on Terrorism, Al Qaeda, and US Policies." As of December 10, 2012:
http://www.worldpublicopinion.org/pipa/pdf/feb09/STARTII_Feb09_rpt.pdf

Lempert, Robert J., et al. (2006), "A General Analytic Method for Generating Robust Strategies and Narrative Scenarios," *Management Science*, April, 514–528.

Lempert, Robert J., Steven W. Popper, and Steven C. Bankes (2003), *Shaping the Next One Hundred Years: New Methods for Quantitative Long-Term Policy Analysis*, Santa Monica, Calif.: RAND Corporation. As of June 10, 2012:
http://www.rand.org/pubs/monograph_reports/MR1626.html

Louie, Marcus A., and Kathleen C. Carley (2008), "Balancing the Criticisms: Validating Multi-Agent Models of Social Systems," *Simulation Modeling Practice and Theory*, 16, 242–256.

Lumina Decision Systems, homepage, 2012. As of December 7, 2012:
http://www.lumina.com/

Morgan, M. Granger, and Max Henrion (1992), *Uncertainty: A Guide to Dealing with Uncertainty in Quantitative Risk and Policy Analysis*, New York: Cambridge University Press.

Nance, Richard E. (1999), "Distributed Simulation with Federations: Expectations, Realizations, and Limitations," *Proceedings of the 1999 Winter Simulation Conferences*, 1026–1031.

National Academy of Sciences (1996), *Post–Cold War Conflict Deterrence*, Washington, D.C.: National Academy Press.

National Research Council (2006), *Defense Modeling, Simulation, and Analysis: Meeting the Challenge*, Washington, D.C.: National Academies Press.

Noricks, Darcy M. E. (2009), "The Root Causes of Terrorism," in *Social Science for Counterterrorism; Putting the Pieces Together*, edited by Paul K. Davis and Kim Cragin, Santa Monica, Calif.: RAND Corporation, 11–70.

Paul, Christopher (2009), "How Do Terrorists Generate and Maintain Support?" in *Social Science for Counterterrorism: Putting the Pieces Together*, edited by Paul K. Davis and Kim Cragin, Santa Monica, Calif.: RAND Corporation, 113–209.

Pearl, Judea, *Causality* (2009), *Models, Reasoning, and Inference*, Cambridge, Mass.: Cambridge University Press.

Popper, Karl R. (1934), *The Logic of Scientific Discovery*, London: Hutchinson, 1934.

Ragin, Charles C. (1989), *The Comparative Method: Moving Beyond Qualitative and Quantitative Strategies*, Berkeley, Calif.: University of California Press.

——— (2000). *Fuzzy-Set Social Science*, Chicago, Ill.: University of Chicago Press.

Rieger, Thomas (2008), *Desperate Measures: Different Types of Violence, Motivations, and Impact on Stability*, Washington, D.C.: Gallup Consulting.

Ritchie, Adelia (ed.) (1992), *Simulation Validation Workshop Proceedings (SIMVAL II)*, Alexandria, Va.: Military Operations Research Society.

Rosenhead, Jonathan, and John Mingers (eds.) (2004), *Rational Analysis for a Problematic World Revisited*, Chichester, UK: John Wiley.

Sargent, Robert G. (2010), "A Perspective on Modeling, Data, and Knowledge," in *Proceedings of Unifying Social Frameworks*, sponsored by the National Academy of Science for the Office of Naval Research. As of December 10, 2012:
http://www7.nationalacademies.org/dbasse/A_Prospective_on_Modeling_Data_and_Knowledge.pdf

Sterman, John D. (2000), *Business Dynamics: Systems Thinking and Modeling for a Complex World*, Boston: McGraw-Hill.

System Architectures Laboratory, homepage, no date. As of December 7, 2012:
http://sysarch.gmu.edu/main/

Tetlock, Philip E. (2005), *Expert Political Judgment: How Good Is It? How Can We Know?* Princeton, N.J.: Princeton University Press.

University of Pittsburgh, GeNIe/SMILE website, no date. As of December 7, 2012:
http://genie.sis.pitt.edu/

Waltz, Ed (2008), "Situation Analysis and Collaborative Planning for Complex Operations," 13th ICCRTS (International Command and Control Research and Technology Symposium), C2 for Complex Operations.

Youngblood, Simone M., et al. (2000), "Simulation Verification, Validation, and Accreditation," *Johns Hopkins Applied Physics Laboratory*, 21, 359–367.

Zeigler, Bernard (1984), *Multifaceted Modeling and Discrete Event Simulation*, Ontario, Calif.: Academic Press.